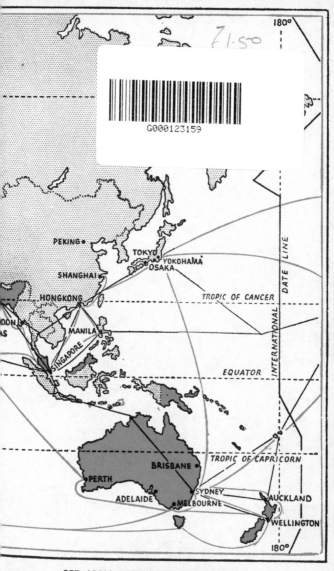

71.50

RED AREAS—BRITISH COMMONWEALTH
ROUTES: BLACK—AIR; RED—SEA

SCHOOLBOY'S
POCKET BOOK

THE SCHOOLBOY'S POCKET BOOK

Edited by
CARLTON WALLACE

EVANS BROTHERS LIMITED

MONTAGUE HOUSE · RUSSELL SQUARE · LONDON

This edition first published 2007 by
Evans Brothers Limited
2A Portman Mansions
Chiltern Street
London W1U 6NR

This special Evans Centenary facsimile edition of the 1958 Schoolboy's Pocket Book is a fascinating glimpse into a boy's world of 50 years ago. Here are the facts and fantasies of the time, providing a nostalgic look back, and a startling reminder of how much has changed in just five decades.

Health and Safety
Please note that this is a facsimile edition of the 1958 Pocket Book. No changes to the text have been made, but the Publishers wish to point out that some of the recipes and other instructions would no longer be recommended today, for health and safety reasons.

British Library Cataloguing in Publication Data is available for this title.

ISBN 9780237534943

© Evans Brothers Limited 1958

Printed and bound in Malta by Gutenberg Press Ltd.

VISIT OUR WEBSITE
Evans
www.evansbooks.co.uk

CONTENTS

Part I—STUDENT'S COMPENDIUM

5

THE BRITISH COMMONWEALTH

LANGUAGE

TABLES AND FORMULÆ

CONTENTS 7

PART II—HOBBIES, PASTIMES, SPORT

LIST OF ILLUSTRATIONS

Part I

STUDENT'S COMPENDIUM

10

Index to Part I

NOTE: The Index to Hobbies, Pastimes, and Sport (Part II) appears on page 122.

THE UNIVERSE

THE VAST SPREAD of heavenly bodies in space, of which the Earth and its Moon are the most important part so far as we are concerned, make up what is known as the Universe. For convenience this Universe is divided into three parts: the Fixed Stars, the Solar System, and the Earth and its Moon. Facts about each of these are set out below.

THE FIXED STARS

Measuring Astronomical Distances

Since the nearest fixed star is some 270,000 times farther away from the Earth than the Sun, and the Sun is about 93 million miles distant, there could be no question of measuring stellar distances in miles; the figures resulting would be so great as to be meaningless, and comparisons would be difficult. For example, the nearest star (Bungula in Centaurus) is about 25,000,000,000,000 miles away.

Until a short time ago the means of measuring stellar distances was the *light-year*; that is, the distance light travels in one year at a speed of rather more than 186,000 miles per second. The light-year thus represents some 6,000,000,000,000 miles.

Today there is a new astronomical unit of measurement known as the *parsec*. Scientifically, the parsec is the distance at which the mean radius of the Earth's orbit would subtend an angle of 1 second (angular measurement); in terms of miles, this distance is a little more than 19,000,000,000,000.

For practical purposes it is convenient to regard 1 parsec as equalling 3¼ light-years.

The Constellations

Examination of the night sky when there is no cloud reveals to the unaided eye about two or three thousand heavenly bodies. If a good pair of binoculars is used, the number

THE NIGHT SKY

In the above map, the North (Pole) Star is in the centre. To find it in the sky, first locate Great Bear (Ursa Major), and trace the Pole Star by means of its "pointers."

The shading represents the relative position of the Milky Way.

will be increased to about a quarter of a million. An observer seated at one of the giant astronomical telescopes (such as that at Mount Wilson, California) could find some 50 million.

Man observed the stars long before he could read or write, and he divided what he saw into groups or *constellations*. In time these constellations began to take on shapes in Man's mind, and eventually he gave those shapes names of common objects—animals, and so on.

The Galaxy, or Milky Way, was the most obvious of the star-groupings, and it can be seen on a fine night spread across the sky in a broad irregular band. Smaller star-groupings which can be observed from various parts of the Earth's surface are given in the list below. In this list the Latin (scientific name) is given first, and then the name by which each constellation was known to the Ancients.

List of Constellations

Andromeda	Chained Lady	Corona	Northern
Antlia	Air Pump	Borealis	Crown
Apis	Bee	Corvus	Crow
Apus	Bird of Paradise	Crater	Cup
		Crux	Southern Cross
Aquarius	Water Carrier		
Aquila	Eagle	Cygnus	Swan
Ara	Altar	Delphinus	Dolphin
Argo	A Ship	Dorado	Sword Fish
Aries	Ram	Draco	Dragon
Auriga	Wagoner	Equuleus	Little Horse
Boötes	Herdsman	Eridanus	Eridanus (River)
Cælum	Sculptor's Tool		
Camelopardus	Giraffe	Fornax	Furnace
Cancer	Crab	Gemini	Twins
Canes Venatici	Hunting Dogs	Grus	Crane
Canis Major	Dog	Hercules	Hercules
Canis Minor	Lesser Dog	Horologium	Clock
Capricornus	Sea-Goat	Hydra	Sea Serpent
Carina	Ship's Keel	Hydrus	Water Snake
Cassiopeia	Lady in the Chair	Indus	India
		Lacerta	Lizard
Centaurus	Centaur	Leo	Lion
Cepheus	Monarch	Leo Minor	Small Lion
Cetus	Whale	Lepus	Hare
Chamæleon	Chameleon	Libra	Balance
Circinus	Compasses	Lupus	Wolf
Columba	Dove	Lynx	Lynx
Coma Berenices	Berenice's Hair	Lyra	Lyre
Corona	Southern	Malux	Ship's Mast
Australis	Crown	Mensa	Table Mountain

Microscopium	Microscope	Sagittarius	Archer
Monoceros	Unicorn	Scorpius	Scorpion
Musca	(Same as Apis)	Sculptor	Sculptor's Studio
Norma	Rule		
Octans	Octant	Scutum Sobieski	Sobieski's Shield
Ophiuchus	Serpent Bearer		
Orion	Giant-Hunter	Serpens	Serpent
Pavo	Peacock	Sextans	Sextant
Pegasus	Winged Horse	Taurus	Bull
Perseus	Rescuer	Telescopium	Telescope
Phœnix	Phœnix	Triangulum	Triangle
Pictor	Easel	Triangulum Australis	Southern Triangle
Pisces	Fish		
Piscis Australis	Southern Fish	Tucana	Toucan
		Ursa Major	Great Bear
Puppis	Ship's Poop	Ursa Minor	Little Bear
Pyxis	(Same as Malus)	Vela	Ship's Sails
		Virgo	Virgin
Reticulum	Net	Volans	Flying Fish
Sagitta	Arrow	Vulpecula	Fox

Stars and their Magnitudes

Stars are roughly classified according to their brightness as seen by an observer on the Earth, and this brightness is given the name *magnitude*. Stars of magnitude 0 to 6 can be seen by the unaided eye, magnitude 0 being the brightest, each succeeding magnitude being about $2\frac{1}{2}$ times less bright.

There are two very bright stars which have been given *minus magnitudes* in the brightness scale because they are brighter than magnitude 0. These stars are shown in the list below.

As a point of interest, the brightness of the Sun is $-26\cdot7$ and the Moon $-11\cdot2$ in terms of star magnitudes.

The Brightest Stars

Name of Star	Constellation	Magnitude	Distance (in parsecs)
Aldebaran	Taurus	1·06	18·0
Altair	Aquila	0·89	4·9
Antares	Scorpio	1·22	38·5
Arcturus	Boötes	0·24	12·5
Betelgeuse	Orion	0·90	59·0
Bungula	Centaurus	0·06	1·3

Canopus	Puppis	−0·86	200·0
Capella	Auriga	0·21	13·0
Castor	Gemini	1·58	13·0
Deneb	Cygnus	1·33	200·0
Formalhaut	Piscis Aust.	1·29	7·3
Markab	Pegasus	2·57	26·0
Polaris*	Ursa Minor	2·12	143·0
Pollux	Gemini	1·21	9·9
Procyon	Canis Minor	0·48	3·2
Regulus	Leo	1·34	17·0
Rigel	Orion	0·34	167·0
Sirius	Canis Major	−1·58	2·7
Spica	Virgo	1·21	111·0
Vega	Lyra	0·14	8·1

* Known better as the North Star.

When tracing any particular constellation or star in the night sky, first find Ursa Major and the Pole Star (see map on page 12), then work out from them the position of the group required. In the map, constellations are named in upright type, individual stars in sloping type.

THE SOLAR SYSTEM

THE SOLAR SYSTEM has as its centre the Sun, around which revolve a number of planets. One of these planets is the Earth.

The Sun may be regarded as a large star moving through space, and the planets are its satellites, just as the moon is the satellite of the Earth.

The diameter of the Sun is 864,000 miles. It revolves about its axis once in 25 days 9 hours, and its surface temperature is between 5,500° and 6,000° C.; interior temperature, 1–14 million °C.

Sun Spots. The surface of the Sun is a mass of white-hot gases, and it sometimes happens that storms occur in these gases just as storms occur in the atmosphere surrounding the Earth. These solar storms are known as Sun Spots, and some of them take the form of cyclones measuring 50,000 miles in diameter—large enough to envelop the whole Earth.

The Planets. There are nine Planets, and details of them are contained in the list below. In connection with the column marked "Mass", the Earth's mass (which is reckoned at 6,000 million million million tons) equals 1.

Name of Planet	Dist. from Sun (millions of miles)	Diameter (miles)	Mass	Length of Day	Length of Year
Mercury	36·0	3,000	0·04	88 d.	0·24 y.
Venus	67·2	7,650	0·83	*	0·62 y.
Earth	92·9	7,927	1·00	24 h.	1·00 y.
Mars	141·5	4,200	0·11	24½ h.	1·88 y.
Jupiter	483·3	88,700	318·00	9¾ h.	11·86 y.
Saturn	886·1	75,000	95·00	10¼ h.	29·46 y.
Uranus	1,782·8	30,900	15·00	10¾ h.	84·02 y.
Neptune	2,793·5	33,000	17·00	15¾ h.	164·79 y.
Pluto	3,666·0	*	*	*	247·70 y.

* Not known.

THE EARTH AND ITS MOON

The Earth

IT HAS already been shown above that the Earth is some 92·9 million miles from the Sun and has a mass of 6,000 million million million tons. It is not quite a true sphere, but an oblate spheroid, slightly flattened at the Poles. The diameter from Pole to Pole is 7,900 miles, and at the Equator 7,927 miles. The circumference at the Equator is 24,910 miles.

The Earth has two movements within the Solar System, and these are:

(1) It revolves round the Sun in an elliptical path, making a complete revolution in 365 days 5 hours 49 minutes and 12 seconds, its speed on its path being 18½ miles per second (66,600 miles per hour).

(2) It spins on its polar axis at a rate of once in 24 hours, giving a speed on the surface at the Equator of very nearly 1,038 miles per hour.

The rotation of the Earth about the Sun is anti-clockwise,

and about its polar axis so that a point on its surface moves in an eastward direction.

The polar axis is not at right angles to the path around the Sun, but inclined to it at an angle of $23\frac{1}{2}°$; this fact, coupled with the fact that the Earth's path is an ellipse, gives rise to the seasons (i.e., to the changes of temperature which, on any part of the Earth's surface, give the effect of Summer and Winter and the intermediate seasons of Spring and Autumn).

For details of the distribution of land and water on the Earth's surface, see *The World's Zones* and *The Continents and Oceans* on page 19.

The Earth has been divided up by geographers into Latitude and Longitude, and any place on the Earth's surface can be fixed accurately by means of these two measurements.

Latitude is indicated by parallels to the Equator. The Equator itself is 0°, and any parallel north of it is marked in degrees, minutes, and seconds, the North Pole being Lat. 90° N. Thus Greenwich stands on Lat. 51° 21′ 38″ N., rather more than halfway between the Equator and the North Pole. Parallels south of the Equator are marked as South Latitude; thus Durban in Natal is almost exactly on Lat. 30° S.

Longitude is indicated by meridians from Pole to Pole. The meridian at Greenwich is 0°, and all longitude west of that meridian to 180° is West Longitude; all longitude eastwards to 180° is East Longitude. A reference to an atlas will show that Durban is on the meridian Long. 31° E. Thus the position of Durban on the Earth's surface can be stated as Long. 31° E., Lat. 30° S. Any other place on the Earth's surface can be fixed similarly.

For the importance of Longitude for telling the time in various parts of the world, see *International Date Line* on page 37 and *World Times at Greenwich Noon* on page 39.

Magnetic North. The Earth is like a huge magnet, with the lines of magnetic force running north and south. But the north pole of this huge magnet (the Magnetic North) is not the same as the North Pole just referred to. Actually Magnetic North changes its position very slightly from year to year, but in the main it is in an area north of Canada just off the western end of Baffin Island, roughly at Long. 97° W. and Lat. 71° N. Because of this slight deviation of Magnetic

North from the North Pole, navigators have to apply to their compass readings a correction known as *Variation* so that their bearings can be transferred to their charts.

The Moon

The Moon is the Earth's satellite. It has a diameter of 2,160 miles, and its average distance from the Earth's surface is 238,900 miles. Its mass is nearly 74 million million million tons; $81\frac{1}{2}$ times less than that of the Earth.

The Moon revolves round the Earth once in 27 days 7 hours 43 minutes, but since it also moves with the Earth through space, it has to travel a little farther each month in order to reach the same relative position with regard to the Earth and the Sun; thus the average time from one new moon to the next is 29 days 12 hours 44 minutes. The speed of the Moon on its orbit round the Earth is roughly 2,300 miles per hour.

The Moon does not spin upon an axis as does the Earth, but always presents the same face (or hemisphere) to observers on the Earth's surface; hence astronomers are not able to examine the "back of the moon" with their telescopes.*

Because the Moon is so near the Earth, it exercises a gravitational pull on the Earth's seas and oceans, and this gives rise to the Earth's tides. The tides are always highest when the Moon and the Sun are so positioned in the sky that they pull together.

There is thought to be no atmosphere, and hence no life, on the Moon. The hemisphere which can be seen is dotted with huge craters and mountains (maximum height about 30,000 feet), and these have been mapped by astronomers. Seen with the unaided eye, these geographical features are so placed that they look something like a face, and this gives rise to the expression "Man in the Moon".

* Attempts are being made to examine this unseen hemisphere by means of "moon shots" fired from the earth. These "moon shots", propelled initially by means of powerful rockets, are containers filled with scientific instruments, which can transmit (by means of coded radio signals) what they "see" back to earth.

THE WORLD

THE WORLD'S ZONES

THE WORLD is divided into five zones according to average temperature at sea level, the coldest zones being at the Poles and the hottest being near to the Equator. These zones are:

Arctic	. . .	from the North Pole to 66° 30′ N.
North Temperate	.	from 66° 30′ N. to 23° 38′ N.
Torrid	. . .	from 23° 38′ N. to 23° 38′ S.
South Temperate	.	from 23° 38′ S. to 66° 30′ S.
Antarctic	. . .	from 66° 30′ S. to the South Pole.

THE CONTINENTS AND OCEANS

THE TOTAL AREA of the surface of the Earth is about 197 million square miles, of which land is about 56 million square miles and water is about 141 million square miles. Thus the proportion of land to water is 1 : 2¼ approximately.

The Continents

The world land-areas can best be divided into five continents plus two special regions (Oceania and the combined Polar Regions). Their sizes and populations are stated below in millions.

Continent	Sq. miles	Populations
Europe	3·8 m.	556 m.
Asia	17·0 m.	1,542 m.
North America (incl. Central America) . . .	8·3 m.	268 m.
South America . . .	7·0 m.	129 m.
Africa	11·7 m.	216 m.
Oceania (Australia, New Zealand, the Pacific Islands)	3·2 m.	18 m.
	51·0 m.	2,729 m.

The Oceans and Great Seas

The water areas of the world can be divided roughly into five oceans and a number of great seas. These, with their areas in millions of square miles, are:

Oceans	Atlantic	31·5	
	Pacific	64·0	
	Indian	28·3	
	Arctic	5·5	
	Antarctic	2·0	
			131·3
Great Seas	Malay (South China)	3·1	
	Central American	1·8	
	Mediterranean	1·1	
	Behring	0·9	
	Okhotsk (East Russia)	0·6	
	East China	0·5	
	Hudson Bay	0·5	
	Japanese	0·4	
	Others	0 9	
			9·8
			141·1

COUNTRIES OF THE WORLD

THE AREAS (in thousands of square miles) and populations (in millions of people) given below are not completely accurate—some countries have not been fully measured and mapped, and some populations have not been fully counted, or if they have the correct totals have not been published. But the errors are slight, and the table is accurate enough for all ordinary purposes. (* indicates British territories.)

Country	Area (1,000 sq. miles)	Population (millions)	National Languages
Europe			
Albania	10·7	1·4	Albanian
Andorra	0·2	(5,200)†	Spanish, French
Austria	34·1	7·0	German
Belgium	11·7	9·0	French, Flemish

Bulgaria	42·8	7·6	Bulgarian
Czechoslovakia	49·7	13·3	Czech
Denmark	16·6	4·5	Danish
Finland	130·0	4·3	Finnish
France	212·7	43·9	French
Germany	143·5	67·9	German
Gibraltar*	(1·75)†	(24,000)†	English, Spanish
Great Britain*	89·0	50·3	English
Greece	50·1	7·5	Greek
Hungary	35·9	9·9	Hungarian
Iceland	40·5	0·2	Norroena
Ireland (Republic of)	26·6	2·9	Erse, English
Italy	150·1	50·0	Italian
Liechtenstein	(62)†	(15,050)†	German
Luxemburg	1·0	0·3	French
Malta, G.C.*	0·1	0·3	Maltese, English
Netherlands	12·9	11·1	Dutch
Norway	124·5	3·5	Norwegian
Poland	119·7	27·5	Polish
Portugal	34·5	9·1	Portuguese
Roumania	91·7	17·5	Roumanian
Spain	189·9	29·1	Spanish
Sweden	173·4	7·3	Swedish
Switzerland	15·9	5·2	French, German, Italian
Turkey (Europe)	9·2	2·3	Turkish
U.S.S.R. (Europe)	2,434·0	147·7	Russian, etc.
Yugoslavia	99·0	18·4	Serbo-Croat-Slovene

Asia

Aden Protectorate*	115·1	0·9	Arabic, Hindustani, English
Afghanistan	250·0	11·0	Persian, Pushtu
Borneo (North)*	29·4	0·3	English, many Eastern
Burma	261·6	19·0	Burmese Shan
Ceylon*	25·3	8·1	Sinhalese, Tamil
China	4,135·0	575·0	Chinese (many dialects)
Cyprus*	3·6	0·5	Greek, Turkish, English
India*	1,220·1	361·0	Many Dravidian, Indo-Aryan, and others
Indonesia	735·3	80·0	Indonesian
Iraq	116·6	6·5	Arabic
Israel	8·1	2·0	Hebrew, Arabic
Japan	147·6	91·2	Japanese
Jordan	30·0	1·4	Arabic
Korea (Chosun)	85·2	28·5	North Chinese
Lebanon	3·9	1·4	Arabic, French

Malaya*	50·8	6·2	English, Malay
Outer Mongolia	625·8	2·1	Mongolian (Sharra)
Pakistan*	361·3	75·8	(See India)
Persia	628·0	18·9	Persian
Philippines	115·6	21·0	English, Spanish
Sarawak*	50·0	0·5	English, many native
Saudi Arabia	913·0	5·0	Arabic
Singapore	0·2	1·3	English, Malay
Syria	70·8	3·6	Arabic
Thailand	200·1	22·8	Siamese
Turkey (Asia)	285·2	21·8	Turkish
U.S.S.R. (Asia)	6,276·0	52·5	Russian, etc.
Yemen	75·0	4·0	Arabic

Africa

Algeria	856·0	10·0	Arabic
Basutoland*	11·7	0·6	Bantu, English, Afrikaans
Bechuanaland*	275·0	0·3	(See Basutoland)
Belgian Congo	910·0	17·7	Bantu
British Cameroons*	34·1	1·4	Bantu, English
British Somaliland*	68·0	0·7	Somali
Egypt	386·2	22·6	Arabic, French, English
Ethiopia	398·0	17·0	Amharic, English, Arabic
Gambia*	4·1	0·3	Wolof, English
Ghana	79·2	4·7	Bantu, English
Kenya*	224·9	6·2	English, Swahili
Liberia	43·0	1·5	English
Libya	810·0	1·1	Arabic
Nigeria*	339·0	34·0	Bantu, English
Rhodesia and Nyasaland	489·3	7·5	Bantu, Swahili, English
Sierra Leone*	27·9	1·8	Bantu, English
S.W. Africa*	317·7	0·4	English, German, Afrikaans, Bantu
Sudan	967·5	10·3	Egyptian, Arabic, Nubian, English
Swaziland*	6·7	0·2	Bantu, English
Tanganyika*	362·7	8·5	Swahili, English
Uganda*	94·0	5·6	Bantu, Swahili, English
Union of S. Africa*	472·7	12·6	English, Afrikaans, and native dialects

Zanzibar*	1·0	0·3	Swahili, Arabic, English

North America

Canada*	3,846	16·0	English, French
Mexico	763·9	28·9	Spanish, Mexican, Indian dialects
United States	2,977·1	171·6	English

Central America and West Indies

Bahamas*	4·4	(131,000)†	English
Barbados*	0·2	0·2	English
Bermuda*	(21)†	(43,000)†	English
Brit. Honduras*	8·9	(81,000)†	English, Spanish
Costa Rica	23·0	1·0	Spanish
Cuba	44·1	6·1	Spanish, English
Dominican Republic	19·3	2·7	Spanish
Guatemala	45·5	2·8	Spanish
Haiti	10·2	3·1	French, Creole French
Honduras	44·3	1·7	Spanish
Jamaica*	4·4	1·6	English
Leeward Islands*	(412)†	0·1	English
Nicaragua	57·1	1·2	Spanish
Panama	28·5	1·0	Spanish
Salvador	13·1	2·4	Spanish
Trinidad & Tobago*	2·0	0·7	English
Windward Islands*	0·8	0·3	English

South America

Argentina	1,080·0	20·1	Spanish
Bolivia	506·8	4 0	Spanish, Indian dialects
Brazil	3,275·5	60 0	Portuguese, French, Italian, German
British Guiana*	83·0	0·5	English, Indian dialects
Chile	286·5	6·9	Spanish
Colombia	440·0	13·0	Spanish
Ecuador	275·9	3·9	Spanish
Falkland Islands*	4·6	(2,250)†	English
Paraguay	149·8	1·4	Spanish, Guarani
Peru	482·1	10·2	Spanish, Quichua
Uruguay	72·2	3·0	Spanish
Venezuela	352·1	6·0	Spanish

Oceania

Australia*	2,975·0	9·7	English
Fiji*	7·1	0·3	English

Gilbert & Ellice			
Islands*	0·3	(39,000)†	English
New Guinea*	91·0	1·7	English
New Hebrides‡	5·7	(54,000)†	English, French
New Zealand*	103·4	2·3	English, Maori
Solomon Islands*	11·5	0·1	English
W. Samoa*	1·1	0·1	English

* British Commonwealth territory.

† Figures in brackets are actual, and not in thousands or millions.

‡ New Hebrides is Anglo-French.

Note: In the Africa section, the language called Bantu is frequently mentioned.   Actually Bantu is a large group of African languages, and the group is broken up into hundreds of local dialects.   Swahili is of the Bantu family, used mainly on the eastern side of Africa.

PRINCIPAL WORLD FEATURES

Largest Islands

Island	Location	Area (*sq. miles*)
Australia	West Pacific	2,974,580
Greenland	North Atlantic	827,300
New Guinea	West Pacific	345,000
Borneo	West Pacific	303,500
Baffin Land	North of Canada	235,000
Madagascar	East Africa	228,300
Sumatra	East Indian	178,000
Great Britain	N.W. Europe	89,126
Honshiu	Japan	87,500
Celebes	West Pacific	72,500
South Island	New Zealand	58,500
Java	East Indies	48,400
North Island	New Zealand	44,500
Cuba	Central America	44,000
Newfoundland	East Canada	42,750
Luzon	Philippine Islands	41,000
Ellesmere	North of Canada	40,500
Iceland	North Atlantic	40,440
Mindanao	Philippine Islands	37,000
Hokkaido	Japan	34,700

Ireland	N.W. Europe	32,600
Novaya Zemlya	North of Russia	30,000
Sakhalin	North of Japan	29,100
Haiti	Central America	28,600
Tasmania	South of Australia	26,215
Ceylon	South of India	25,400
Tierra del Fuego	South America	18,500
Spitsbergen	North of Norway	15,260
Hainan	South of China	14,200
Formosa	East of China	13,800
Vancouver	West Canada	12,400
Sicily	South of Italy	10,000

Ocean Deeps

Name	Location	Greatest Depth (in feet)
Mindanao Deep	Philippine Islands	35,948
Nero Deep	Off Guam, Pacific	31,600
Penguin Deep	North of New Zealand	30,940
Tonga Deep	South of Samoa, Pacific	30,300
Puerto Rico Deep	North of Puerto Rico, Caribbean	30,145
Tuscarora Deep	East of Japan	27,850
Kurile Deep	East of Japan	27,800
Virgin Deep	West Indies	27,500
Brazil Deep	Atlantic on Equator	20,700
Sherard Osborne Deep	South of E. Indies	20,100

There are several Deeps in mid-Atlantic towards Canada and the United States which have not been named. One is 22,950 feet.

Longest Rivers

Name	Location	Length (miles)
Missouri-Mississippi	United States	4,500
Nile	Egypt and Sudan	4,160
Amazon	Brazil	4,050
Yangtse	China	3,750
Yenisei	Western Siberia	3,300
Congo	Central Africa	3,300

Lena	Central Siberia	2,850
Mekong	French Indo-China	2,800
Obi	Russia in Europe	2,700
Niger	West Africa	2,650
Hwang Ho	China	2,600
Amur-Saghalin	South-east Siberia	2,500
Parana	Brazil and Argentina	2,450
Volga	Russia in Europe	2,400
Mackenzie	Canada	2,350
La Plata	Argentina	2,300
Yukon	Alaska	2,100
St. Lawrence	Canada	1,800
Rio Grande del Norte	United States and Mexico	1,800
Sao Francisco	Brazil	1,800
Danube	Europe	1,725
Euphrates	Iraq	1,700
Indus	Pakistan	1,700
Brahmaputra	Tibet, India	1,680
Zambesi	Rhodesia, Mozambique	1,600
Ganges	India	1,500

Inland Seas and Lakes

Name	Location	Area (sq. miles)
South China Sea	Far East	3,137,000
Mediterranean Sea	Europe	1,145,000
Behring Sea	Alaska, Siberia	878,000
Gulf of Mexico	North America	800,000
Okhotsk Sea	Eastern Siberia	582,000
Hudson Bay	Canada	500,000
Sea of Japan	Japan, China	405,000
Caribbean Sea	West Indies	231,000
North Sea	North-west Europe	221,000
Red Sea	Africa, Arabia	178,000
Caspian Sea	Russia, Iran	170,000
Black Sea	Russia, Turkey	170,000
Baltic Sea	Scandinavia	166,400
Persian Gulf	Persia	75,000
Lake Superior	Canada	31,820
Lake Victoria Nyanza	Africa	26,300
Aral Sea	Turkestan	24,400

Lake Huron	United States	23,000
Lake Michigan	United States	22,500
Lake Chad	N.E. Nigeria	20,000
Lake Nyasa	N. Mozambique	14,250
Lake Tanganyika	Tanganyika	12,700
Great Bear Lake	Canada	11,660
Lake Baikal	Siberia	11,600
Great Slave Lake	Canada	11,200

Great Waterfalls

Name	Location	Height (ft.)
Angel Falls	Venezuela	3,212
Yosemite Falls	Yosemite Park, California	2,560
Sutherland Falls	South Island, New Zealand	1,900
Wollomombie Falls	New South Wales	1,700
Ribbon Fall	Yosemite Park, California	1,610
Uitshi Fall	British Guiana	1,230
Takakaw Fall	Canada	1,200
Gersoppa Falls	Mysore, Southern India	960
Chirombo Fall	Tanganyika	880
King Edward VIII Fall	British Guiana	840
Victoria Falls	Southern Rhodesia	400
Glomach Fall	Ross-shire, Scotland	370
Niagara Falls	Lakes Erie and Ontario, Canada	167

Note: Although Niagara Falls have no very great height, they are some 3,000 feet wide, and are the greatest in the world for sheer volume of water going over them.

Highest Mountains

Name	Range	Location	Height (ft.)
Everest	Himalayas	India, Tibet	29,002
Godwin-Austen	Himalayas	India, Tibet	28,250
Kinchinjanga	Himalayas	India, Tibet	28,146
Makalu	Himalayas	India, Tibet	27,790
Nanga Parbat	Himalayas	India, Tibet	26,630
Tengri Khan	Alai Mts.	Turkestan	24,000
Aconcagua	Andes	Argentina	22,976
Illimani	Andes	Bolivia	21,221
Chimborazo	Andes	Ecuador	20,498

McKinley	Alaska	Alaska	20,300
Cotopaxi	Andes	Ecuador	19,612
Mount Logan	Rockies	Yukon, Canada	19,539
Mount Elias	Rockies	Yukon, Canada	19,500
Potro	Andes	Chile	19,355
Kilimanjaro	Tanganyika	Tanganyika	19,340
Elburz	Elburz	Persia	18,562
Demavend	Elburz	Persia	18,464
Tolima	Andes	Colombia	18,320
Charles Louis	Charles Louis	Dutch New Guinea	18,000
Popocatapetl	Mexican	Mexico	17,540
Ararat	Ararat	Eastern Turkey	17,160
Mont Blanc	Alps	France	15,782

Active Volcanoes

Name	Range	Location	Height (ft.)
Cotopaxi	Andes	Equador	19,612
Mount Wrangell	Alaska	Alaska	14,000
Mauna Loa		Hawaii	13,675
Erebus	Ross	Antarctica	13,000
Iliamna		Aleutian Islands	11,000
Chillan	Andes	Chile	10,500
Ruapehu		New Zealand	9,175
Paricutin	Mexican	Mexico	9,000
Asama-yama	Kuishiu	Japan	8,200
Hecla		Iceland	5,100
Kilauea		Hawaii	4,090
Vesuvius		Italy	3,700
Stromboli	Lipari	Italy	3,000

Land Areas Below Sea Level

(Figures in brackets show greatest depth in feet below Sea Level)

Europe:	Zuider Zee, Netherlands (16)
Asia:	Dead Sea, Palestine (1,292)
	Turfan Basin, Sinkiang, China (980)
	Caspian Sea, U.S.S.R.-Iran (84)
	Oman-Qatar, Eastern Arabia (70)

Africa:	Kattara, Lower Egypt (about 500)	
	Faiyum, Lower Egypt (150)	
	Salt Plains, Eritrea (380)	
	Shott Melghir, Algeria (90)	
America:	Death Valley, California (275)	
	Salton Sink, California (245)	
Australia:	Lake Eyre, South Australia (40)	

Great Tunnels

Tunnel	Location	Purpose	Length (miles)
Croton	New York, U.S.A.	Water supply	38
New Croton	,, ,,	,, ,,	31
Shandaken	,, ,,	,, ,,	18
City-Northern	London	Railway	17½
West-End Northern	London	Railway	16
Ben Nevis	Scotland	Water supply	15
Florence Lake	California, U.S.A.	Water supply	13
Simplon	Switzerland	Railway	12½
Bologna–Florence	Italy	Railway	11½
St. Gotthard	Switzerland	Railway	9¼
Loetschberg	Switzerland	Railway	9
Cascade	S. Dakota, U.S.A.	Railway and Water	8
Mont Cenis	S. France	Railway	7¾
Arlberg	Austria	Railway	6¼
Moffat	Colorado, U.S.A.	Railway	6
Otira	S. Island, New Zealand	Railway	5¼
Connaught	British Columbia, Canada	Railway	5
Hohe Tauern	Austria	Railway	5
Somport	Pyrenees, Spain	Railway	5
Ste. Marie-aux-Mines	E. France	Railway	4½
Rove	S. France	Canal traffic	4½
Severn	England	Railway	4¼
Totley	England	Railway	3½
Queensway	Liverpool, England	Road traffic	2¾

Famous Bridges

The lengths of the bridges given below are in feet over the
waterways in each case. The actual length of a bridge-
system, including approach roads, is often very much greater.
For example, the Triborough Bridge system of New York is
about 16 miles long, and consists of four bridges covering
17,710 feet of waterway. The Key West system in Florida
is 130 miles in length, and covers 17¼ miles of water by means
of a number of separate bridges erected between islands.
The San Francisco (Oakland) Bridge is 87 miles long, although
the actual waterway spans are only about 3 miles. And
finally, the Hardinge Bridge (listed below) is, with its approach
structures, some 15 miles long.

Name of Bridge	Location	Waterway Length (feet)
Zambesi	N. Mozambique	11,322
Storsstromsbroen	Denmark	10,500
Tay	Dundee, Scotland	10,289
Upper Sone	Bihar, India	9,839
Godavari	Madras, India	8,880
Forth	Edinburgh, Scotland	8,289
Rio Salado	Buenos Aires, Argentina	6,640
Golden Gate	San Francisco, U.S.A.	6,450
Hardinge	R. Ganges, India	5,900
Rio Dulce	North Argentina	5,866
Victoria Jubilee	Montreal, Canada	5,275
Moerdijk	Dordrecht, Netherlands	4,625
Jacques Cartier	Montreal, Canada	3,950
Queensborough	New York, U.S.A.	3,850
George Washington	New York, U.S.A.	3,500
Brooklyn	New York, U.S.A.	3,450
Torun	West Poland	3,420
Little Belt (Storsstromsbroen)	Denmark	2,707
St. Louis	Missouri, U.S.A.	2,000
Sydney Harbour	New South Wales, Australia	1,650
Menai	North Wales	1,510

Ship Canals

There is a difference between ship canals and ordinary
canals. The former can take cargo ships, while the latter are

only wide and deep enough for barge traffic. Barge canals sometimes run for hundreds of miles, but in the list below ship canals only are mentioned.

Canal	Country	Joining	Length (miles)
Gota	Sweden	Stockholm and Gothenburg	115
Suez	Egypt	Mediterranean and Red Seas	100
Moscow	U.S.S.R.	Moscow and Leningrad	80
Albert	Belgium	Antwerp and Liege	80
Kiel	Germany	North and Baltic Seas	61
Panama	Panama	Atlantic and Pacific Oceans	50
Elbe	Germany	Magdeburg and Berlin	41
Manchester	England	Mersey Estuary and Manchester	35
Welland	Canada	Lakes Erie and Ontario	26
Amsterdam	Netherlands	North Sea and Zuider Zee	16½
Corinth	Greece	Gulfs of Corinth and Ægina	4

Tallest Buildings

Name of Building	Location	Storeys	Height (feet)
Empire State	5th Avenue, N.Y.	102	1,470
Chrysler	Lexington Ave., N.Y.	77	1,046
Eiffel Tower	Champ de Mars, Paris	—	985
Cities Service	Wall St., N.Y.	67	950
Bank of Manhattan	Wall St., N.Y	70	927
R.C.A. Building	6th Avenue, N.Y.	70	850
Woolworth	Broadway, N.Y.	60	792
City Bank Farmers' Trust	William & Beaver St., N.Y.	60	760

(There are 28 other buildings in New York which are between 760 and 500 feet in height)

University Building	Pittsburg, U.S.A.	42	535
Pyramid of Cheops	Gizeh, Egypt	—	450
Cathedral	Salisbury, England	—	404
St. Paul's Cathedral	London, England	—	365

Principal Capital Cities

The populations given in this list are to the nearest thousand, and are approximate only. City populations are changing constantly, and it is not possible to say just how many people are living in any one of them at any particular time.

Country	Capital	Population (thousands)
Europe		
Albania	Tirana	50
Austria	Vienna	1,614
Belgium	Brussels	993
Bulgaria	Sofia	726
Czechoslovakia	Prague	972
Denmark	Copenhagen	960
Finland	Helsinki	403
France	Paris	2,850
Germany, Western	Bonn	140
Eastern	Berlin	1,200
Great Britain	London	8,346
Greece	Athens	1,200
Hungary	Budapest	1,850
Iceland	Reykjavik	66
Ireland	Dublin	540
Italy	Rome	1,853
Luxemburg	Luxemburg	68
Malta, G.C.	Valetta	19
Netherlands	Amsterdam	871
Norway	Oslo	447
Poland	Warsaw	996
Portugal	Lisbon	784
Rumania	Bucharest	1,237
Spain	Madrid	1,869
Sweden	Stockholm	794
Switzerland	Berne	161
U.S.S.R.	Moscow	4,900
Yugoslavia	Belgrade	510
Asia		
Afghanistan	Kabul	300
Burma	Rangoon	740

Ceylon	Colombo	425
China	Peking	2,800
Cyprus	Nicosia	82
India	Delhi	1,100
Indonesia	Djakarta	260
Iraq	Bagdad	552
Israel	Jerusalem	149
Japan	Tokyo	8,774
Jordan	Amman	250
Korea	Seoul	1,575
Lebanon	Beirut	450
Malaya	Kuala Lumpur	300
Pakistan	Karachi	1,126
Persia	Tehran	1,500
Philippines	Manila	1,181
Saudi Arabia	Riyadh	100
Syria	Damascus	372
Thailand	Bangkok	1,773
Turkey	Ankara	353

Africa

Algeria	Algiers	361
Angola	St. Paul de Loanda	40
Belgian Congo	Leopoldville	370
Egypt	Cairo	2,100
Ethiopia	Addis Ababa	400
Gambia	Bathurst	21
Ghana	Accra	136
Kenya	Nairobi	100
Liberia	Monrovia	41
Nigeria	Lagos	320
Rhodesia and Nyasaland	Salisbury	216
Sierra Leone	Freetown	65
Sudan	Khartoum	93
Tanganyika	Dar es Salaam	129
Uganda	Entebbe	8
Union of S. Africa	Pretoria	343
	Cape Town	729
Zanzibar	Zanzibar	45

S P.B.—3

North America

Canada	Ottawa	222
Mexico	Mexico City	4,227
United States	Washington D.C.	800

Central America

Bahamas	Nassau	50
Barbados	Bridgetown	18
Bermuda	Hamilton	3
Brit. Honduras	Belize	22
Costa Rica	San José	128
Cuba	Havana	783
Dominican Republic	Ciudad Trujillo	273
Guatemala	Guatemala	285
Haiti	Port au Prince	196
Honduras	Tegucigalpa	100
Jamaica	Kingston	162
Nicaragua	Managua	108
Panama	Panama	128
Salvador	San Salvador	188
Trinidad	Port of Spain	120

South America

Argentina	Buenos Aires	3,733
Bolivia	La Paz	339
Brazil	Rio de Janeiro	2,950
Chile	Santiago	1,628
Colombia	Bogotá	872
Ecuador	Quito	229
Paraguay	Asuncion	207
Peru	Lima	1,050
Uruguay	Montevideo	900
Venezuela	Caracas	1,102

Oceania

Australia	Canberra	37
Fiji	Suva	32
Hawaii	Honolulu	292
New Zealand	Wellington	140

Great Merchant Ships

Name	Nationality	Gross Tons	Length (ft.)
Q. Elizabeth	British	83,673	1,031
Q. Mary	British	81,237	1,019
United States	United States	53,329	917
Liberté	French	51,839	937
Ile de France	French	44,356	793
Nieuw Amsterdam	Netherlands	36,667	753
Mauretania	British	35,674	771
Caronia	British	34,183	715
Pasteur	German	30,447	697
Arcadia	British	29,734	721
Iberia	British	29,614	718
Cristoforo Colombo	Italian	29,191	700
Orsova	British	28,790	722
Edinburgh Castle	British	28,705	747
Pretoria Castle	British	28,705	747
Pendennis Castle	British	28,500	763
Orcades	British	28,164	709
Himalaya	British	27,955	709

CALENDARS OF THE WORLD

The Roman Calendar was devised from one supposed to have been invented by Romulus, said in mythology to have founded the city of Rome in 753 B.C. The first Roman year was of 304 days divided into 10 months. Later someone added two more months, and the year then consisted of 12 months of 29 and 30 days alternately, plus an extra day, making 355 days in all. Since this arrangement did not coincide with a true year (one complete revolution of the Earth round the Sun), the Roman Calendar resulted in much confusion after some hundreds of years, and it gave way to the Julian Calendar.

The Julian Calendar was worked out by Sosigenes, an Egyptian astronomer, and put into force by Julius Cæsar in 45 B.C. It fixed the average length of the year at 365¼ days, which resulted in a loss of 11 minutes 10 seconds every year. This loss mounted as hundreds of years went by, again resulting in confusion.

The **Gregorian Calendar** eventually put the matter right, and it is the Calendar used by nearly the whole of the world today. It was introduced by Pope Gregory XIII in 1582, and established the year at 365 days 5 hours 49 minutes 12 seconds. England did not adopt the Calendar until 1752, by which time the reckoning by the old Calendar was 11 days too much; thus, when the Gregorian Calendar came into force, 11 days had to be dropped altogether. This led to some trouble because many people thought that they were being robbed of 11 days of life; but eventually everybody settled down to the new way of reckoning.

Leap Year. Our present ordinary calendar year consists of 365 days, and in order to allow for the hours, minutes and seconds unaccounted for, the Leap Year of 366 days was invented. This happens every 4th year, in years which can be divided by 4, except that unless century-years (i.e., 1800, 1900, 2000) can be divided by 400 they are not considered as Leap Years.

There are other Calendars which are used for special purposes side by side with the Gregorian Calendar. These are:

The **Jewish Calendar,** which is calculated from the supposed date of the Creation (set at 3,760 years and 3 months before the birth of Christ). The ordinary Jewish year has 354 days, and is made up of 12 months. Every 19 years, however, there are 7 years of 384 days, and this adjustment brings the Jewish Calendar into line with the regular solar year. The Jewish months have 30 and 29 days alternately, and are called Tishri, Hesvan, Kislev, Tebet, Sebat, Adar, Nisan, Yiar, Sivan, Tamuz, Ab, and Elul; in years of 384 days an extra month of 30 days, called Veadar, is inserted after Adar. The Jewish New Year's Day comes some time between September 5 and October 5 in the Gregorian Calendar.

The **Moslem Calendar** is used in some parts of India, Malaya, Arabia, Persia, and Egypt, and is reckoned from the flight of Mohammed from Mecca to Medina on July 16, A.D. 622 (called the Hejira). The Moslem year has an average length of 354 days 8 hours 48 minutes, and is divided into 12 months of 30 and 29 days alternately. There is a cycle of 30 years, 19 of which have 354 days and 11 have 355 days, the extra day being added to the last month of the year. Since this method of calculation does not correspond to the solar year, months and seasons do not always correspond.

The Coptic Calendar is used by people in parts of Ethiopia and Egypt, and is of 365 days made up of 12 months of 30 days each plus 5 extra (holiday) days for 3 years and 6 extra days for every 4th (Leap) year.

SEVEN WONDERS OF THE WORLD

THERE are two recognised sets of Seven Wonders of the World—that of Antiquity and that of the Middle Ages. They are—

The Seven Wonders of Antiquity: 1, The Pyramids of Egypt; 2, The Hanging Gardens of Babylon; 3, The Tomb of Mausolus (Halicarnassus, Asia Minor); 4, The Temple of Diana (near Smyrna, now Izmir); 5, The Colossus of Rhodes; 6, The Statue of Jupiter (Greece); 7, The Pharos of Egypt.

The Seven Wonders of the Middle Ages: 1, Colosseum of Rome; 2, The Catacombs of Alexandria; 3, The Great Wall of China; 4, Stonehenge; 5, The Leaning Tower of Pisa; 6, The Porcelain Tower of Nanking; 7, The Mosque of St. Sophia (Constantinople, now Istanbul).

THE INTERNATIONAL DATE LINE

PLACES east of Greenwich have times which are fast of Greenwich Mean Time, and places west have times which are slow, the difference being 1 hour for each 15° of longitude (see *World Times at Greenwich Noon* on page 39).

On the other side of the world, crossing the Pacific from north to south, there is the meridian of 180° longitude, and it is here that two adjacent days of the calendar meet.

To make this clear, if two travellers can go so fast that they can reach the 180° meridian from Greenwich in a few seconds, and both start off in opposite directions at midnight on a Thursday, then the one who goes westward (across the Atlantic) will arrive at 180° some 12 hours earlier by local time; that is, at about noon on Thursday. The other, going eastwards (across Europe and Russia), will arrive at the same spot some 12 hours later by local time; that is, at noon on Friday. Thus, although they have taken but a few seconds on their respective journeys, there is a day difference between them by calendar when they arrive. Hence it is said that adjacent days meet at 180° longitude.

So that there should be no muddle over this, an International Date Line has been established. For most of its length it follows the 180° meridian, but it varies slightly so that it runs through the middle of the Behring Strait, then to the east of the Aleutian Islands; later it goes westwards of the Fiji, Tonga, and Chatham Islands. You can see its course on the map at the end of this book.

A captain of a ship or aircraft crossing the I.D. Line puts his calendar back a day when going in an easterly direction, and forward a day when going in a westerly direction.

SUMMER TIME

IN BRITAIN, the idea of putting the clock forward one hour during the summer months first took effect in 1916. The purpose of this arrangement was at first to save power for lighting, and later (in peacetime) to enable people to enjoy longer summer evenings in the open.

During the last war, the idea was extended during the years 1941 to 1945, the clock being put forward two hours for part of the summer.

Summer time begins each year at 2 a.m. on the day following the third Saturday in April, but if that day be Easter Day, then a week earlier. It ends at 2 a.m. on the day following the first Saturday in October. In any year these dates may be varied or Double Summer Time (two hours forward) may be introduced by special Order in Council.

Other places have adopted systems of Summer Time. Amongst these are: Albania, Azores, Bermuda, Brazil, British Honduras, Canada (Yukon excepted), China (parts only), Formosa, Hong Kong, Hungary, Iceland, Indo-China, Ireland (Republic of), Israel, Korea, Macao, Madagascar, Madeira, Morocco, Pescadores Islands, Poland, Portugal, U.S.A. (parts only).

WORLD TIMES AT GREENWICH NOON

NEARLY all places in the world have two times—local standard time (which is the time shown on local clocks) and longitude time (the time worked out at the rate of one hour for each 15 degrees of longitude east or west of Greenwich).

The second kind of time is useful mainly to sailors and airmen, who have to know about longitude in order to fix their positions when making voyages and flights. It would not be convenient to use this kind of time on land.

For example, when it is noon at Greenwich it is only 11.40 a.m. (20 minutes earlier) at Falmouth by longitude time. The Falmouth clocks would show noon, however, and so would the clocks in every other place in Britain, no matter what its longitude. Thus there is no muddle over time in places within the country which are only a few miles apart.

But Britain is small compared with some countries. In the United States, for example, the country is divided into time-zones, and when it is 7 a.m. in New York by the clocks, it is only 4 a.m. in San Francisco (three hours earlier).

In the table below are shown the principal cities of the world in the first column, the local standard (clock) time in the second, and the longitude time in the third, when it is noon at Greenwich. The 24-hour clock is used, and figures less than 12 are a.m., while figures more than 12 are p.m.

Adelaide	. .	21.30	21.14		
Aden	. .	15.00	13.1		
Alexandria	.	14.00	13.59		
Algiers	. .	12.00	12.12		
Amsterdam	.	13.00	12.19		
Antwerp	. .	12.00	12.17		
Athens	. .	14.00	13.33		
Auckland	.	24.00	23.40		
Bâle	. .	13.00	12.31		
Baltimore	.	7.00	6.44		
Belfast	. .	12.00	11.35		
Berlin	. .	13.00	12.54		
Bermuda	.	9.00	7.40		
Berne	. .	13.00	12.30		
Bombay	. .	17.30	16.51		
Borneo	. .	20.00	19.40		
Boston	. .	7.00	7.15		
Boulogne	.	12.00	12.15		
Brindisi	. .	13.00	13.12		
Brisbane	.	22.00	22.13		
Brussels	.	12.00	12.18		
Bucharest	.	14.00	13.45		
Buenos Aires	.	8.00	8.7		
Cairo	. .	14.00	14.5		
Calcutta	.	18.00	17.53		
Canton	. .	20.00	19.33		
Cape Town	.	14.00	13.13		
Chicago	. .	6.00	6.10		

Christchurch, N.Z. . .	24.00	23.32
Colombo . .	17.30	17.13
Concepcion (Chile) . .	7.00	7.8
Constantinople.	14.00	13.56
Copenhagen .	13.00	12.50
Delagoa Bay .	14.00	14.12
Dublin . .	12.00	11.35
Durban . .	14.00	14.2
Edinburgh .	12.00	11.48
Genoa . .	13.00	12.36
Gibraltar .	12.00	11.29
Guatemala .	6.00	5.58
Halifax, Nova Scotia . .	8.00	7.45
Hamburg . .	13.00	12.40
Havana . .	7.00	6.30
Hobart . .	22.00	21.48
Hong Kong .	20.00	19.35
Honolulu . .	2.00	1.20
Jamaica . .	7.00	6.55
Kabul . .	16.55	16.55
Karachi . .	17.30	16.28
Leningrad .	15.00	14.1
Lima . .	7.00	6.52
Lisbon . .	12.00	11.24
Madeira . .	11.00	10.55
Madras . .	17.30	17.21
Madrid . .	12.00	11.45
Malta . .	13.00	12.58
Manila (Philippine Is.) . .	20.00	20.3
Mecca . .	14.40	14.40
Melbourne .	22.00	21.40
Mexico City .	5.00	5.25
Monte Video .	8.30	8.15
Montreal . .	7.00	7.6
Naples . .	13.00	12.57

Newfoundland .	8.30	8.30
New Orleans .	6.00	6.1
New York . .	7.00	7.4
Odessa . .	15.00	14.1
Oslo . .	13.00	12.40
Panama . .	7.00	6.42
Paris . .	12.00	12.10
Penang . .	19.30	18.42
Pernambuco .	9.00	9.40
Perth, W.A. .	20.00	19.40
Pretoria . .	14.00	13.54
Quebec . .	7.00	7.15
Rangoon . .	18.30	18.20
Rio de Janeiro	9.00	9.8
Rome . .	13.00	12.50
Salonica . .	14.00	13.32
San Francisco .	4.00	3.50
Santiago . .	7.00	7.20
Shanghai . .	20.00	20.5
Singapore . .	19.30	18.55
Smyrna . .	14.00	13 49
Stockholm . .	13.00	13.12
Suez . .	14.00	14.11
Sydney . .	22.00	22.5
Tangier . .	12.00	11.36
Tokyo . .	21.00	21.20
Toronto. .	7.00	6.42
Trinidad . .	8.00	7.54
Tripoli . .	13.00	12.53
Valparaiso . .	7.00	7.15
Vancouver . .	4.00	3.55
Vienna . .	13.00	13.5
Washington, D.C. . .	7.00	6.42
Wellington . .	24.00	23.38
Winnipeg . .	6.00	5.32
Zanzibar . .	15.00	14.37
Zürich . .	13.00	12.34

FOREIGN MONEY

IN THE TABLE below are shown foreign monetary units (the monetary unit of Britain is the £ sterling), then the value of each unit in terms of £ s. d., and finally the number of each unit the £ will buy.

The values of foreign money in relation to that of Britain change somewhat from time to time, and the figures given are intended only as a rough guide. A bank will always give the exact day-to-day value of any particular foreign money if asked.

Country	Monetary Unit	Value in £ s. d.	No. to £
Argentina	Peso	1·5d.	156
Australia	Australian £	16s.	1·25
Austria	Schilling	3·3d.	72
Belgium	Belgian franc	1·7d.	140
Bolivia	Boliviano	125 for 1d.	30,000
Brazil	Cruzeiro	0 56d.	430
Bulgaria	Lev	1s. 0¾d.	19
Burma	Kyat	1s. 6d.	13·33
Canada	Dollar	7s. 4d.	2·75
Ceylon	Rupee	1s. 6d.	13·33
Chile	Peso	9·4 for 1d.	2,250
China	Yuan	2s. 11d.	6·9
Colombia	Peso	11d.	22
Costa Rica	Colon	1s. 4d.	15·75
Cuba	Dollar	7s. 2d.	2·8
Czechoslovakia	Crown	1s.	20
Denmark	Krone	12·4d.	19·3
Dominican Republic	Dollar	7s. 2d.	2·8
Ecuador	Sucre	5½d.	42·5
Egypt	Egyptian £	20s. 6d.	97·5*
Finland	Mark	0·27d.	900
France	Franc	0·2d.	1,175
Germany	Mark	1s. 8d.	11·75
Greece	Drachma	3d.	84
Guatemala	Quetzel	7s. 2d.	2·8
Haiti	Gourde	1s. 5d.	14

* Per £100.

Honduras	Lempira	3s. 7d.	5·6
Hong Kong	Silver dollar	1s. 3d.	16
Iceland	Krona	5·3d.	45
India	Rupee	1s. 6d.	13·33
Indo-China	Piastre	2·4d.	98
Indonesia	Rupiah	2·9d.	83
Iraq	Dinar	£1	1
Israel	Israeli £	£1	1
Italy	Lira	7·3 for 1d.	1,750
Japan	Yen	4·2 for 1d.	1,008
Lebanon	Lebanon £	2s. 3d.	9
Luxembourg	Franc	1·7d.	140
Madagascar	Franc	0·4d.	590
Malaya	Silver dollar	2s. 4d.	8·6
Mexico	Peso	7d.	35
Netherlands	Florin	1s. 10½d.	10·65
New Zealand	New Zealand £	£1	1
Nicaragua	Cordoba	1s.	19·6
Norway	Krone	1s.	20
Pakistan	Rupee	1s. 6d.	13·33
Panama	Balboa	7s. 2d.	2·8
Paraguay	Guarani	0 8d.	306
Persia	Rial	1d.	230
Peru	Sol	3¼d.	67·5
Philippines	Peso	3s. 7d.	5·6
Poland	Zlote	1s. 9½d.	11·2
Portugal	Escudo	3d.	80
Rhodesia	Rhodesian £	£1	1
Roumania	Leu	1s. 2d.	17
Salvador	Colon	2s. 10d.	7
Spain	Peseta	2d.	120
Sweden	Krona	1s. 4d.	14·5
Switzerland	Franc	1s. 7½d.	12.25
Thailand	Baht	4½d.	55
Turkey	Turkish £	10d.	25
Union of South Africa	S. African £	£1	1
United States	Dollar	7s. 2d.	2·8
U.S.S.R.	Rouble	1s. 9½d.	11·2
Uruguay	Peso	11d.	23
Venezuela	Bolivar	2s. 2d.	9·35
Yugoslavia	Dinar	0·28d.	840

THE BRITISH COMMONWEALTH

AREA AND POPULATION

THE BRITISH Commonwealth of Nations consists of ten independent nations as named below, plus their Colonies, Protectorates, and so on, plus the new Federation of Rhodesia and Nyasaland. All (except India, which is now a Republic with its own President) acknowledge Her Majesty Elizabeth II as their Queen. The area and estimated population of the Commonwealth are shown in the table below; for details of local areas, populations, and languages, see *Countries of the World* on page 20 (where British territories are marked *) and for capitals see *Capital Cities* on page 32.

Continent	Area (sq. miles)	Population
Europe (including the Mediterranean Area)	125,350	51,000,000
Asia	2,346,000	457,000,000
Africa	4,650,000	86,600,000
North America	3,894,000	16,000,000
Central America (including the West Indies)	21,000	3,300,000
South America	98,000	525,000
Oceania	3,300,000	16,000,000
Totals	14,434,350	630,425,000

The Nations are actually self-governing and entirely independent, but are united voluntarily by a common loyalty to the Crown. They are: Australia, Canada, Ceylon, Ghana, India, Malaya (Federation of), New Zealand, Pakistan, the Union of South Africa, United Kingdom.

The Colonies, Protectorates, etc., are sometimes self-governing; some have Assemblies which can regulate or advise upon their internal affairs, but final authority is in the hands of the government in London. They are: Aden, Bahamas, Bermuda, British Guiana, British Honduras, Cyprus, Falkland Islands, Fiji, Gambia, Gibraltar, Hong Kong, Kenya, Malta GC, Mauritius, Nigeria, North Borneo, St. Helena, Sarawak, Seychelles, Sierra Leone, Singapore, Somaliland, Uganda, West Indies (Federation of: Antigua and Barbuda, Barbados, Dominica, Grenada, Jamaica, Montserrat, St. Kitts-Nevis-Anguilla, St. Lucia, St. Vincent, Trinidad and Tobago), Western Pacific Islands (Solomons, Gilbert and Ellice, etc.), Zanzibar.

Other Territories. There are a few territories which are considered as International Trusteeships, and for whose safety and well-being the United Nations is primarily responsible. The United Nations has granted the administration of these territories to the British Commonwealth: British Cameroons, Nauru Island, New Guinea, Tanganyika, Western Samoa.

The following Independent States continue to act under the advice of the British Government: Brunei, Tonga.

The New Hebrides is jointly administered by Great Britain and France. New Guinea and Papua are looked after by Australia, W. Samoa by New Zealand, and Nauru Island by Britain, Australia, and New Zealand jointly.

MONARCHS OF BRITAIN

Until 1301, Wales was considered as an independent kingdom having its own sovereigns. In that year the son of Edward I of England was created Prince of Wales, and in 1307 he became King of England and Wales.

Before the Union of the Crowns of England and Scotland in 1603, Scotland was also an independent kingdom.

And before the year 827, England itself was not a united country, but had separate kings for areas like Wessex, Mercia, and so on. In 827 there ascended to the throne the "first King of all the English"—Egbert the Great, King of Wessex, who subdued the other kingdoms mainly by force. Thereafter the English Monarchs were as follow:

English Kings

Name	Descent	Came to Throne
Saxon		
Ethelwulf	Son of Egbert the Great	839
Ethelbald and Ethelbert	Sons of Ethelwulf	858
Ethelred I	Third son of Ethelwulf	866
Alfred the Great	Fourth son of Ethelwulf	871
Edward the Elder	Son of Alfred the Great	901
Athelstan	First son of Edward the Elder	925
Edmund I the Magnificent	Third son of Edward the Elder	940
Edred	Fourth son of Edward the Elder	946
Edwy	Son of Edmund	955
Edgar the Peaceable	Second son of Edmund	958
Edward the Martyr	Son of Edgar	975
Ethelred II the Unready	Son of Edgar	979
Edmund II (Ironside)	Son of Ethelred	1016
Danish		
Canute	(By conquest)	1017
Harold I	Son of Canute	1035
Hardicanute	Son of Canute	1040
Saxon		
Edward the Confessor	Son of Ethelred II	1042
Harold II	Brother of Edith, wife of Edward the Confessor	1066
Norman		
William I of Normandy	(By conquest)	1066
William II	Son of William I	1087
Henry I	Son of William I	1100
Stephen	Son of fourth daughter of William I	1135
Plantagenet		
Henry II	Son of daughter of Henry I	1154
Richard I	Son of Henry II	1189

John	Son of Henry II	1199
Henry III	Son of John	1216
Edward I	Son of Henry III	1272

England and Wales

Edward II	Son of Edward I	1307
Edward III	Son of Edward II	1327
Richard II	Grandson of Edward III	1377

Lancaster

Henry IV	Grandson of Edward III	1399
Henry V	Son of Henry IV	1413
Henry VI	Son of Henry V	1422

York

Edward IV	Great-grandson of Edward III	1461
Edward V	Son of Edward IV	1483
Richard III	Brother of Edward IV	1483

Tudor

Henry VII	Son of Edmund Tudor, who was the son of Owen Tudor and Katherine, the widow of Henry V	1485
Henry VIII	Son of Henry VII	1509
Edward VI	Son of Henry VIII	1547
Jane	Grand-daughter of Mary, sister of Henry VIII	1553
Mary I	Daughter of Henry VIII	1553
Elizabeth I	Daughter of Henry VIII	1558

Great Britain
Stuart

| James I | (King James VI of Scotland) | 1603 |
| Charles I | Son of James I | 1625 |

(Here came Oliver Cromwell, 1653–8, and Richard Cromwell, 1658–9)

| Charles II | Son of Charles I | 1660 |
| James II | Son of Charles I | 1685 |

William III	Son of William of Orange and Mary, daughter of Charles I	}1689
Mary II	Daughter of James II	
Anne	Daughter of James II	1702

Hanover

George I	Son of Elector of Hanover and Sophia, grand-daughter of James I	1714
George II	Son of George I	1727
George III	Grandson of George II	1760
George IV	Son of George III	1820
William IV	Son of George III	1830
Victoria	Grand-daughter of George III	1837

Saxe-Coburg

Edward VII	Son of Victoria	1901

Windsor

George V	Son of Edward VII	1910
Edward VIII	Son of George V	1936
George VI	Son of George V	1936
Elizabeth II	Daughter of George VI	1952

Sovereign Princes of Wales (844 to 1282)

Rhodri the Great	844	Gruffydd ap Llywelyn	1039
Anarawd	878	Bleddyn	1063
Hywel Dda	916	Trahaern	1075
Iago ab Ieuaf	950	Gruffydd ap Cynan	1081
Hywel ab Ieuaf	979	Owain Gwynedd	1137
Cadwallon	985	Dafydd ab Owain	1170
Maredudd	986	Llywelyn Fawr	1194
Cynan	999	Dafydd ap Llywelyn	1240
Llywelyn ap Sitsyhlt	1018	Llywelyn ap Gruffydd	1246
Iago ab Idwal	1023		

(Llywelyn ap Gruffydd died in 1282, and Edward, the son of Edward I of England, became the first English Prince of Wales in 1301. Since then the eldest son of the ruling monarch has generally been created Prince of Wales. The present Prince of Wales is Prince Charles, son of Queen Elizabeth II.)

Kings of Scotland (1057 to 1603)

The dates given are those on which the respective rulers began their reigns.

Malcolm I . . .	1057	David II	1329
Donald	1093	Robert II . . .	1371
Duncan	1094	Robert III . . .	1390
Donald (restored to throne) . . .	1095	James I	1406
Edgar	1097	James II	1437
Alexander I . . .	1107	James III . . .	1460
David I	1124	James IV	1488
Malcolm II . . .	1153	James V	1513
William	1165	Mary (Queen of Scots)	1542
Alexander II . . .	1214	(Mary reigned from	
Alexander III . .	1249	1542 to 1567, when	
Margaret . . .	1286	she was forced to	
John Balliol . . .	1292	abdicate)	
Robert I (the Bruce) .	1306	James VI	1567

(James VI of Scotland, son of Mary Queen of Scots, became James I of Britain in 1603.)

THE ROYAL FAMILY

Queen Elizabeth II (the Queen Regnant) is the elder daughter of the late King George VI. She was born in London on April 21, 1926, and on November 20, 1947, married the Duke of Edinburgh (formerly Prince Philip of Greece, and a great-great-grandson of Queen Victoria). She succeeded to the Throne on the death of her father on February 6, 1952. Her Majesty has two children: Prince Charles Philip Arthur George, Heir Apparent to the Throne, born on November 14, 1948; and Princess Anne Elizabeth Alice Louise, born at Clarence House, London, on August 15, 1950.

The Queen Mother is the daughter of the 14th Earl of Strathmore and Kinghorne, and was born on August 4, 1900, being given the names Elizabeth Angela Marguerite Bowes-Lyon. On April 26, 1923, she married the Duke of York, second son of King George V, and upon the abdication of King Edward VIII (now Duke of Windsor) and the accession of the Duke of York to the Throne on December 11, 1936, she became Queen. She has two children: Queen Elizabeth II (see above); and Princess Margaret Rose, who was born at Glamis Castle, Angus, Scotland, on August 21, 1930.

Succession to the Throne

The order of succession to the Throne is now:
Prince Charles (see above).
Princess Anne (see above).
Princess Margaret (see above).

The Duke of Gloucester (Henry William Frederick Albert), brother of the late King, born March 31, 1900. He married Lady Alice Montagu-Douglas-Scott on November 6, 1935.

Prince William Henry Andrew Frederick of Gloucester, son of above, born December 18, 1941.

Prince Richard Alexander Walter George, brother of Prince William, born August 26, 1944.

Then follow the Duke of Kent (born October 9, 1935), Prince Michael of Kent (born July 4, 1942), Princess Alexandra of Kent (born December 25, 1936), The Princess Royal (born April 25, 1897), and The Earl of Harewood (born February 7, 1923).

BRITISH FLAGS

The Royal Standard of the British Isles is the personal flag of Her Majesty, and may be flown only when she is actually present in a building. It must never be flown when she is passing in procession. The flag is divided into 4 quarters. The 1st and 4th quarters each contain the three lions passant of England, the 2nd quarter contains the lion rampant of Scotland, and the 3rd quarter contains the harp of Ireland.

The Union Flag of the British Isles, more generally known as The Union Jack, is the flag which may be flown by all Her Majesty's subjects. It was introduced in 1606 following the union of England and Scotland, and it now contains in one design the red and white cross of St. George, the blue and white cross of St. Andrew, and the red and white cross of St. Patrick. The Union Jack is flown correctly when the larger strips of white next to the flagstaff are uppermost.

The White Ensign is the flag of the Royal Navy and the

Royal Yacht Squadron. It consists of a white flag bearing the cross of St. George, with a small Union Jack in the top corner next to the flagstaff.

The Red Ensign is the flag flown by all British merchant vessels not belonging to the Royal Navy. It is a plain red flag with the Union Jack in the top quarter next to the flag-staff, and is known amongst sailors as "the red duster".

The Blue Ensign is the flag of the Royal Naval Reserve and of certain yacht clubs whose names are shown in the Navy List. It is similar to the Red Ensign, but the background colour is blue.

Most countries and territories of the British Common-wealth have their own flags, but in many cases a Union Jack will be found in the top quarter next to the flagstaff. The notable exception is the Union of South Africa, which has a flag of orange, white, and blue in equal horizontal bars with a device of small flags in the middle of the white, these small flags including the Union Jack and the flag of the Netherlands.

THE BRITISH CONSTITUTION

The Crown, which consists of The Queen at the head of the High Court of Parliament, is the responsible authority of Central Government. The Queen opens Parliament every year by making a speech from the Throne in the House of Lords, and thereafter she conducts the day-to-day business of State through her Privy Council. The Queen entrusts executive duties to her Ministers.

The Cabinet is formed of the Ministers of the Crown, and usually consists of 17 Ministers, not more than 15 of whom may be Members of the House of Commons. There may also be 23 Parliamentary Secretaries, of whom not more than 21 may be Members of the House of Commons, and not less than 2 must be Members of the House of Lords. The head of the Cabinet is the Prime Minister, who is appointed personally by the Queen.

The House of Lords consists of royal princes, archbishops, marquesses, earls, viscounts, bishops, barons, and law lords; it is presided over by the Lord High Chancellor. The right to sit in the House of Lords is governed by elevation to a peerage or by birth.   In 1958, peeresses became eligible to sit in the House of Lords for the first time in history.   The House of Lords must, in theory, approve of all Bills intended to become Acts of Parliament passed by the House of Commons (except money Bills, of which the Budget is the most important) before the Queen will sign them and make them law.   If the House of Lords refuses to approve any Bill, the Bill may still go forward to the Queen for signature after one year if the House of Commons puts it forward again.   The House of Lords also forms a Court of Appeal (the highest in the land), which consists of 7 law lords and some others who have held legal appointments.   The decisions of this Court become law.

The House of Commons consists of 630 citizens who have been elected as Members of Parliament by their fellow-citizens.   Its proceedings are governed by rules called Standing Orders, and directed by a chairman (called the Speaker) who is elected by the Members themselves.   The House as last elected at a General Election may continue for 5 years, after which Parliament is declared dissolved and there has to be another General Election.   In theory no Member of the House of Commons may resign, but he must cease to be a Member when he is appointed to an office under the Crown; hence, in order to resign he applies for a job known as the Stewardship of the Chiltern Hundreds.   This job has no duties or salary, but it is an office under the Crown, hence anyone appointed to it is no longer allowed to be a Member.

Nearly all Members of the House of Commons belong to one or other of the political parties of the day, and when, after a General Election, one party is found to have more Members elected to the House than any other, that party becomes the Government.   From it the Queen appoints her Prime Minister, and the Prime Minister appoints other Ministers, some of whom form the Cabinet.

The Government will remain in office until, by vote, it is defeated in the House on some important issue; it is then called upon to resign its powers, which may be taken up by the next largest party.   Alternatively, if the next party feels it is likely to be defeated by vote very soon after it forms a Government, the Prime Minister advises the Queen to dissolve Parliament, and there has to be a General Election, whether 5 years since the last General Election have passed or not.

How Our Laws Are Made

ONE OF the most important functions of Parliament is to make laws whereby the country's affairs may be regulated. While any proposed law is being discussed and shaped, it is called a Bill; when it finally receives the Queen's Assent, it becomes an Act of Parliament.

A Bill may be drafted and introduced either by the Government or by any Member of either House. Most Bills are introduced in the House of Commons, where they go through the following stages:

First Reading. The Bill is formally introduced in the House, and ordered to be printed so that everyone shall know its contents.

Second Reading. The principles of the Bill are explained by the Minister or other Member who introduced it, and the House usually debates it and then decides, often by vote, whether it shall go any further. If the supporters of the Bill are in the majority, the Bill goes to—

Committee, where it is examined closely, clause by clause and word by word, and altered or "amended."

Report Stage. After the Committee has reported to the House, further amendments may be made by the House.

Third Reading. The Bill, as amended, is discussed by the House, and accepted or rejected as a whole. If it is accepted, it goes to the House of Lords, where it passes through procedure similar to that described above.

The House of Lords may accept, amend or reject the Bill —unless it is a Finance Bill (which contains the Budget proposals) or any other Bill certified by the Speaker to be a "Money" Bill. Since 1911, the Lords have by law had to pass such Bills without amendment.

A Bill passed by the Lords without amendment is ready for the Royal Assent, which is signified by Commissioners who act for the Queen. If it is amended it goes back to the House of Commons for the amendments to be considered; and if the Commons agree to the amendments, the Bill is ready for the Royal Assent.

If the Lords reject a Bill introduced in the Commons, it cannot be put forward for Royal Assent. If, however, the House of Commons pass a Bill in two successive Sessions and the House of Lords reject it each time, the Bill goes forward for Royal Assent provided that there is a year's interval between the Second Reading in the Commons in the first Session and the Third Reading in the Commons in the second Session.

Britain's Prime Ministers

The official residence of the Prime Minister of the day is No. 10 Downing Street, just off Whitehall in London. His country residence is Chequers, near Princes Risborough, Bucks.

The Prime Ministers, from Sir Robert Walpole (who is generally considered to have been the first), are as follow:

Prime Minister	Party	Date	Prime Minister	Party	Date
Sir Robert Walpole	Whig	1721	Viscount Melbourne	Whig	1834
Earl of Wilmington	Whig	1742	Sir Robert Peel	Tory	1834
Henry Pelham	Whig	1743	Vct. Melbourne	Whig	1835
Duke of Newcastle	Whig	1754	Sir Robert Peel	Tory	1841
Duke of Devonshire	Whig	1756	Lord John Russell	Whig	1846
Duke of Newcastle	Whig	1757	Earl of Derby	Tory	1852
Earl of Bute	Tory	1762	Earl of Aberdeen	Peelite	1852
George Grenville	Whig	1763	Viscount Palmerston	Lib.	1855
Marquess of Rockingham	Whig	1765	Earl of Derby	Cons.	1858
Duke of Grafton	Whig	1766	Vct. Palmerston	Lib.	1859
Lord North	Tory	1770	Earl Russell	Lib.	1865
M. of Rockingham	Whig	1782	Earl of Derby	Cons.	1866
Earl of Shelburne	Whig	1782	Benjamin Disraeli	Cons.	1868
Duke of Portland	C.	1783	E. W. Gladstone	Lib.	1868
William Pitt	Tory	1783	B. Disraeli	Cons.	1874
Henry Addington	Tory	1801	W. E. Gladstone	Lib.	1880
William Pitt	Tory	1804	Marquess of Salisbury	Cons.	1885
Lord Grenville	Whig	1806	W. E. Gladstone	Lib.	1886
Duke of Portland	Tory	1807	M. of Salisbury	Cons.	1886
Spencer Perceval	Tory	1809	W. E. Gladstone	Lib.	1892
Earl of Liverpool	Tory	1812	Earl of Rosebery	Lib.	1894
George Canning	Tory	1827	M. of Salisbury	Cons.	1895
Viscount Goderich	Tory	1827	A. J. Balfour	Cons.	1902
Duke of Wellington	Tory	1828	Sir H. Campbell-Bannerman	Lib.	1905
Earl Grey	Whig	1830	H. H. Asquith	Lib.-C.	1908

D. Lloyd George	C.	1916	N. Chamberlain	C.	1937
A. Bonar Law	Cons.	1922	Winston Churchill	C.	1940
S. Baldwin	Cons.	1923	C. R. Attlee	Lab.	1945
J. R. Macdonald	Lab.	1924	Sir Winston		
S. Baldwin	Cons.	1924	Churchill	Cons.	1951
J. R. Macdonald	Lab.-C.	1929	Sir Anthony Eden	Cons.	1955
S. Baldwin	C.	1935	Harold Macmillan	Cons.	1957

Note: Cons.=Conservative; C.=Coalition; Lib.=Liberal;
Lab.=Labour.

GOVERNMENT DEPARTMENTS

THE DAY-TO-DAY organisation and management of the
country is in the hands of the Civil Service, which is
divided into a number of Departments. Each Department
is headed by a Minister or some other person responsible
for its conduct to Parliament.

The list below shows the principal Government Departments,
the responsibilities of each, and the Parliamentary head.

Admiralty, Board of (Whitehall, London)—The Royal Navy
and the guarding of British ships and sea routes; First
Lord of the Admiralty

Agriculture, Fisheries and Food, Ministry of (Whitehall Place
London)—All matters related to farming, fishing, animal
health, agricultural research, plant and fish diseases,
ordnance survey and the supply and distribution of food;
Minister.

Air Ministry (Adastral House, London)—The Royal Air Force
and the guarding of British aircraft and air routes; Secretary of State.

Commonwealth Relations Office (Downing Street, London)—
Relations with the independent nations of the British
Commonwealth; Secretary of State.

Colonial Office (Gt. Smith Street, London)—The administration of the Colonies; Secretary of State.

Defence, Ministry of (Storey's Gate, London)—Co-ordin-
ating and advising upon all matters of defence and combined operations (involving the Admiralty, War Office, Air
Ministry, Ministry of Labour, Ministry of Supply, and so
on); Minister.

Education, Ministry of (Curzon Street, London)—The administration of State schools and education generally; Minister.

Foreign Office (Downing Street, London)—The conduct of relations with foreign powers and the control of those parts of Germany and Austria occupied by British forces; Secretary of State for Foreign Affairs.

Health, Ministry of (Saville Row, London)—Matters concerning health, hospitals, and nursing; Minister.

Home Office (Whitehall, London)—Communications from the King to the people, the maintenance of law and order, the enforcement of Acts of Parliament, and the maintenance of civil defence, fire, immigration, police, prison and similar services; Secretary of State for Home Affairs.

Housing and Local Government, Ministry of (Whitehall, London)—Controls housing, water supplies, and sewerage, the use of land; supervises and helps to finance local government; Minister.

Labour and National Service, Ministry of (St. James's Square, London)—Maintenance of services to help people train for and obtain employment, maintenance of registers of employers and employees, registration and calling up of National Service men and their resettlement after their service has been completed, matters relating to industrial health and the inspection of factories, dealing with industrial relations and the employment of foreign labour; Minister.

Pensions and National Insurance (John Adam Street, London)—National insurance, war pensions, family allowances, industrial injuries insurance, National Assistance Board; Minister.

Post Office (St. Martins le Grand, London)—The collection, conveyance, and delivery of all postal packets and telegrams, the maintenance of national and international telephone services, the collection of national insurance revenue and the payment of allowances and pensions, the management of post office savings facilities; Postmaster-General.

Power (Millbank, London)—Production and consumption of coal, gas, electricity, petrol, oil, iron and steel; Minister.

Scottish Office (Whitehall, S.W.1)—Everything which concerns Scotland; Secretary of State for Scotland.

Supply, Ministry of (Strand, London)—Munitions of war, military aircraft, atomic energy and research, and the supply of heavy raw materials for war industry; Minister.

Board of Trade (Horse Guards Avenue, London)—All matters concerning the industry and commerce of the United Kingdom which are not covered by the Ministries of Agriculture, Fisheries and Food, Supply, and Works, and all matters affecting patents, the registration of companies, and bankruptcy; President of the Board of Trade.

Transport and Civil Aviation (Berkeley Square, London)—Railways, merchant shipping, canals, roads and road transport, bridges, ferries, harbours, docks, pilotage, lighthouses, coastguards, wreck and salvage, all non-military aircraft and air transport, aerodromes, air training, and aids to air navigation: Minister.

Treasury (Gt. George Street, London)—All matters relating to national finance, the Civil Service; Prime Minister and First Lord of the Treasury.

Works, Ministry of (Albert Embankment, London)—Government and other public buildings, parks, monuments, building, civil engineering and building materials; Minister.

DATES TO REMEMBER EACH YEAR

Movable

Easter Day can fall at any time in any year between March 22 and April 25, it being fixed as the first Sunday after the full moon which happens on or immediately after March 21. Maundy Thursday is the Thursday and Good Friday is the Friday before Easter Day, and the day following Easter Day is a Bank Holiday. Shrove Tuesday (Pancake Day) is always the Tuesday in the seventh week before Easter.

Whit Sunday is always the seventh Sunday after Easter, and the day following it is a Bank Holiday. Whit Sunday thus must come between May 10 and June 13 in any year.

August Bank Holiday is always the first **Monday in** August.

Fixed

Jan. 1—New Year's Day	**Jul.** 4—Independence
26—Foundation Day	Day (U.S.)
(Australia)	**Aug.** 4—Queen Mother's
Feb. 14—St. Valentine's Day	Birthday.
Mar. 1—St. David's Day	**Sept.** 26—Dominion Day
17—St. Patrick's Day	(N.Z.)
Apl. 1—All Fools' Day	**Oct.** 21—Trafalgar Day
21—The Queen's Birthday	24—United Nation's
23—St. George's Day	Day
May 24—British Common-	31—All Hallow's Eve
wealth Day	**Nov.** 10—Lord Mayor's Day
31—Union Day (S.	14—Prince Charles's
Africa)	Birthday.
Jun. 2—Coronation Day	*27—Thanksgiving Day
10—Prince Philip's	(U.S.)
Birthday.	30—St. Andrew's Day
13—Queen's Official	**Dec.** 25—Christmas Day
Birthday (1957)	26—Boxing Day
Jul. 1—Canada Day	31—New Year's Eve

* *For 1958—otherwise the last Thursday in November.*

DISTANCES BY SEA AND AIR

THE DISTANCES shown below of certain important places from England are by the usual routes of ordinary travel, and are in miles.

England to	By Sea	By Air
Australia—Sydney	12,039	13,200
Brazil—Rio de Janeiro	5,034	5,500
Burma—Rangoon	7,590	7,041
Canada—Montreal	2,760	2,800
Denmark—Copenhagen	683	651
Egypt—Alexandria	2,954	2,308
Far East—Hong Kong	9,373	9,830
France—Marseilles	1,839	658
India—Bombay	5,915	5,360
India—Calcutta	7,587	6,386

Iraq—Basra	6,053	3,465
Kenya—Mombasa/Nairobi . . .	5,984	4,945
Malaya—Singapore	7,933	8,393
New Zealand—Wellington . . .	12,309	14,435
Pakistan—Karachi	5,728	4,880
Sweden—Stockholm	1,092	1,028
Tunisia—Tunis	2,045	1,280
Union of South Africa—Cape Town	5,947	7,904
United States—New York . . .	3,043	3,000

BRITAIN'S MONEY

THE MONETARY UNITS which are legal tender (i.e., good for making payments) in Britain at the present time are:

Gold: Coins of £5, £2, £1 (sovereign), and 10s. (half-sovereign) which bear the date 1838 or later.

Bank of England Notes: £5, £1, 10s.

"Silver": Coins of 5s. (crown), 4s. (double-florin), 2s. 6d. (half-crown), 2s. (florin), 1s. (shilling), 6d. (sixpence), 4d. (groat), 3d. (threepence), 2d. (twopence), and 1d. (penny) which bear the date 1816 or later.

Nickel-Brass: 3d. (twelve-sided).

"Copper": 1d. (penny), ½d. (halfpenny), and ¼d. (farthing) which bear the date 1860 or later.

The notes and coins most in circulation are £5, £1, 10s., 2s. 6d., 2s., 1s., 6d., 3d., 1d., ½d., and ¼d. All the others are extremely scarce.

Gold

The only £5 and £2 gold coins likely to be found now are those bearing the date 1937; about 5,500 of each were struck to commemorate the coronation of King George VI.

The last sovereigns for ordinary circulation to be struck bear the date 1917, and the last half-sovereigns the date 1915.

Since the gold in each of these coins (91% of the total coin-weight) is worth far more than the face value, it is very unlikely that anyone will offer the coins as ordinary legal tender.

Bank of England Notes

There was a time when these notes could be issued for almost any amount, and values were printed for £1,000, £500 and many others down to £5. Below £5, the notes were issued by the Treasury and called Treasury Notes.

Now all notes of legal tender are Bank of England Notes (the Bank acting as financial agents for the Treasury), and any notes above the value £5 ceased to be legal tender in May 1945.

"Silver"

Until 1920, silver coins contained $92\frac{1}{2}\%$ of silver; in that year the silver was reduced to 50%; and in 1946 the "silver" coins became cupro-nickel (half copper, half nickel).

The present crowns were struck in 1952-3, the last double-florins in 1890, and the last groats for general circulation in 1856. The present 4d., 3d., 2d., and 1d. pieces in silver are issued as Maundy Money only, and are very rare.

Nickel-brass

Because the old silver 3d. bit was so unpopular (it was very small and easily lost), a new twelve-sided 3d. bit was first issued in 1937, and is now in general circulation. (Nickel-brass=79 parts of copper, 20 parts of zinc and 1 part nickel.)

"Copper"

These "copper" coins are really bronze (95 parts of copper, 4 parts of tin, and 1 part of zinc), and the first in present circulation as legal tender are dated 1860.

Making Payments

Gold and notes as stated above are legal tender for any amount. "Silver" is legal tender up to a total of £2 (that is, if you offer more than that sum in "silver" in payment for anything, it can be refused and notes demanded); and "copper" is legal tender up to 1s.

The twelve-sided threepenny piece is legal tender up to 2s.

Legal Weights

Bronze coins should weigh as follow: pennies, 3 to the ounce; halfpennies, 5 to the ounce; farthings, 10 to the ounce (avoirdupois).

SHIPS OF THE ROYAL NAVY

THE PRINCIPAL SHIPS of the Royal Navy are divided into the following main classes: Battleship, Aircraft Carriers, Cruisers, Daring Class, Destroyers, Anti-Submarine and Mine-Laying. No indication of their armaments can be given.* Some of the ships of each class are as follow:

Name	Completed	Displacement (tons)	Speed (knots)
Battleship			
Vanguard	1946	44,500	30
Aircraft Carriers			
Ark Royal	1955	43,050	32
Victorious	1941	30,500	31
Albion	1954	23,200	25
Magnificent	1948	15,700	25

(Eagle is similar to Ark Royal; Centaur and Bulwark are similar to Albion.)

Cruisers			
Superb	1945	8,000	31·5

(Swiftsure, Ceylon, Newfoundland, Bermuda, Gambia, Jamaica, Kenya, and Mauritius are similar to Superb.)

Belfast	1939	10,000	32·5
Birmingham	1937	9,000	32

(Newcastle and Sheffield are similar to Birmingham.)

Daring Class

All of 2,800 tons; speed, 34·75 knots.

Daring (1952), Defender (1952), Diamond (1952), Duchess (1952), Dainty (1953), Decoy (1953), Delight (1953), Diana (1954).

Destroyers

Agincourt	1947	2,460	35·75

(Aisne, Alamein, Barrosa, Corunna, Dunkirk, Jutland, and Matapan are similar to Agincourt.)

Armada	1945	2,315	35·75

(There are 12 other destroyers similar to Armada.)

Battleaxe	1947	2,000	34·75

(Broadsword, Crossbow, and Scorpion are similar to Battleaxe.)

Anti-Submarine and Minelaying

Childers	1945	2,050	36·75
Caesar	1944	1,700	36·75

(There are 19 other vessels in this class similar to Caesar).

* Many ships of the Royal Navy are constantly being modified in order to be able to carry new types of armaments, such as unguided and guided missiles, as well as (or in place of) guns and torpedoes.

In recent years many large Submarines and Anti-Submarine Frigates have been completed, and others are under construction.

DECORATIONS FOR GALLANTRY

The Victoria Cross (V.C.), founded in 1856, is a bronze cross inscribed "For Valour", and awarded to anybody who was acting under the direction of the Armed Forces and performed an act of great gallantry in the presence of the enemy. The ribbon is claret.

The George Cross (G.C.), founded in 1940, is a silver cross inscribed "For Gallantry", and awarded to anybody who performed an act of great gallantry at any time, whether under direction of the Armed Forces or in the presence of the enemy or not. The ribbon is dark blue.

The Distinguished Service Order (D.S.O.) is awarded only to officers of the Armed Forces or the Merchant Navy. The ribbon is red with narrow blue edges.

The Distinguished Service Cross (*D.S.C.*) is awarded to officers of the Royal and Merchant Navies below the rank of Captain, and to W.R.N.S. and R.A.F. flying officers of equivalent rank. The ribbon is blue, white, blue in equal vertical stripes.

The Military Cross (*M.C.*) is awarded to officers of the Army below the rank of Lt. Colonel and R.A.F. ground officers of equivalent rank. The ribbon is white, purple, white in equal vertical stripes.

The Distinguished Flying Cross (*D.F.C.*) is awarded to officers who performed acts of gallantry while engaged in flying operations against an enemy, and may be won by officers of all services. The ribbon is white with purple diagonal stripes.

The Air Force Cross (*A.F.C.*) is awarded to anybody who performs an act of gallantry while flying, but not in the presence of an enemy. The ribbon is white with red diagonal stripes.

The Distinguished Conduct Medal (*D.C.M.*) is the equivalent of the Distinguished Service Order for N.C.Os. and men of the Army and the R.A.F. (ground duties only). The ribbon is red, blue, red in equal vertical stripes.

The Conspicuous Gallantry Medal (*C.G.M.*) is awarded to ranks below that of officer in the Royal Navy, the Royal Marines, the Merchant Navy, and the W.R.N.S. for acts of conspicuous gallantry in the face of the enemy. The ribbon is white with dark blue edges.

The Conspicuous Gallantry Medal (*Flying*) is awarded to ranks below that of officer in the R.A.F. and Army for conspicuous gallantry in the face of the enemy while flying. The ribbon is light blue with dark blue edges.

The Distinguished Service Medal (*D.S.M.*) is awarded to ranks below that of officer in the Royal Navy, Royal Marines, and Merchant Navy for acts of bravery under fire. The ribbon is blue with two white stripes separated by a narrow blue stripe.

The Military Medal (*M.M.*) is awarded to ranks below that of officer in the Army and R.A.F. (ground duties). The ribbon is blue with two crimson and three white stripes alternating in the centre.

The Distinguished Flying Medal (*D.F.M.*) is awarded similarly to the Distinguished Flying Cross, but to ranks below that of officer. The ribbon is white with narrow purple stripes.

The Air Force Medal (A.F.M.) is awarded similarly to the Air Force Cross, but to ranks below that of officer. The ribbon is white with narrow red stripes.

The George Medal (G.M.) is awarded similarly to the George Cross, but where the act of gallantry does not quite merit the Cross. The ribbon is red with five narrow blue stripes.

The British Empire Medal (B.E.M.) is awarded for meritorious service generally, and is open to anybody. The ribbon is pink with narrow grey edges; Service personnel have an additional narrow grey stripe in the centre.

Any of the above Decorations can be won by anybody of any age provided that, where required, he is qualified by rank, service, etc.

LANGUAGE

PARTS OF SPEECH

ALL WORDS are divided into classes according to their use, and those classes are called "parts of speech". In the English language there are eight parts of speech, as follow:

Nouns. Words used to name something (from *nomen*—name).

Adjectives. Words used before nouns to qualify them in some way (from *adjectivus*—that is added to).

Pronouns. Words used instead of or to avoid repeating a noun (from *pro*—instead of; *nomen*—name).

Verbs. Words which state something, as an action (from *verbum*—word).

Adverbs. Words which modify a verb (from *ad verbum*—to a word).

Prepositions. Words which show how things are related to other things (from *prae-positus*—placed before).

Conjunctions. Words which join together words or sentences (from *con-juncto*—joining together).

Interjections. Words additional to a complete sentence which express an emotion (from *inter-jectus*—thrown between).

In the above list, the derivations are all Latin. The parts of speech are the same for most European languages.

Nouns

Gender. Nouns are divided into Masculine (male sex), Feminine (female sex), Common (either sex), and Neuter (neither sex). Examples are: boy, girl, friend, pen.

Number. Nouns can also be Singular (one of anything) or Plural (more than one of anything). Examples: box, boxes; man, men; child, children.

Classes. There are two main classes of nouns: Proper (a name of one particular person or thing), and Common (a name of a group of things). Examples: John, dog. Common nouns are also divided into: Ordinary (denoting a class of things), Collective (denoting a number of things forming one body), and Abstract (denoting some action or quality). Examples: tree, herd, biology.

Cases. These are the different forms which a noun (or a pronoun, the substitute for a noun) assumes to denote its relation to other words in a sentence. The three cases in English are Nominative (which denotes the person or thing about which we are speaking), Objective (which denotes the person or thing to which something is done), and Possessive (which denotes that something belongs to a person or thing). Examples: John (nominative) lives in London (objective); John's (possessive) books are at school.

Note: The Objective case includes the Accusative (direct object) and Dative (indirect object). The Possessive case is also called Genitive.

Adjectives

The adjectives also include the Articles and Numerals.

Degrees of Comparison. There are three degrees of comparison: Positive (simple adjective), Comparative (which compares one thing with another), and Superlative (compares one thing with many and asserts that it possesses greater qualities). Examples: high, higher, highest; bad, worse, worst.

Articles. There are two articles: Definite (indicating one precise thing) and Indefinite (indicating one of a number of things). Examples: the man, a man.

Numerals. The numerals are best indicated by the examples which follow each type: Cardinal (one, two, three), Ordinal (first, second, third), Multiplicatives (once, twice, thrice), and Indefinite (few, many, several).

Pronouns

Since a pronoun is a substitute for a noun, it has gender, number, and case.

Pronouns are divided up as follows: Personal (I, we, you); Demonstrative (this, these); Interrogative (who, what); Relative (that, which); Indefinite (one, none, some); Distributive (each, either); Reflexive (myself, themselves).

Verbs

English verbs are classified in a number of ways, as can be seen from the headings below.

Transitive and Intransitive. A transitive verb is one which in some way affects an object (example: shut the door); an intransitive verb cannot affect an object (example: the door shuts).

Voice. The two voices are Active (example: I shut the door) and Passive (example: The door was shut by me).

Mood. There are three finite moods and the infinitive mood. The finite moods are Indicative (the door is shut); Imperative (shut that door!); and Subjunctive (shut the door so that there will not be a draught). Infinitive mood (to shut the door is better than to leave it open).

Gerund. This is a verbal noun (the shutting of the door).

Participles. There are two participles: the Present or Imperfect (the door is shutting) and the Past (the door was shut).

Tenses. There are twelve tenses, each with an active and passive voice. The first eight tenses listed below are of indicative mood; the last four are of subjunctive mood.

Tense	Active	Passive
Present (Indicative)	I love	I am loved
Past	I loved	I was loved
Present Perfect	I have loved	I have been loved
Past Perfect	I had loved	I had been loved
Future	I shall love	I shall be loved
Future Perfect	I shall have loved	I shall have been loved
Future in the Past	I should love	I should be loved
Future Perfect in the past	I should have loved	I should have been loved

Present (Subjunct-		
ive)	I love	I be loved
Present Perfect	I have loved	I have been loved
Past	I loved	I were loved
Past Perfect	I had loved	I had been loved.

Regular and Irregular. Verbs are divided into Regular (or Weak) and Irregular (or Strong). Verbs that form their past indefinite by adding -ed, -d, or -t (treat, treated) are regular; verbs which do not add a suffix but modify a vowel to form the past indefinite (cling, clung) are irregular.

Adverbs

Adverbs are generally divided according to their meaning, thus:

Adverbs of Quality, such as: well, badly, likewise.

Adverbs of Quantity, such as: nearly, enough, almost.

Adverbs of Relation, such as: (time) now, before, soon; (place) firstly, there, inside; (cause) therefore, accordingly.

Note: Adverbs are nearly always formed from adjectives, often by simply adding the suffix -ly.

Prepositions

Prepositions are classified as Simple and Compound.

Simple. These are: at, by, for, from, in, of, off, on, through, till, to, up, with.

Compound. A few examples of these are: aboard, along, before, between, beyond, except, inside, outside, towards, underneath.

Conjunctions

There are two kinds of conjunctions: Co-ordinative and Subordinative.

Co-ordinative. These join sentences which, without the conjunction, are complete in themselves. Examples: and . . . and, but, either . . . or, neither . . . nor, because, for, as whether.

Subordinative. These join subordinate clauses to a main clause; that is, they join a sentence to another on which it is dependent. Example: He'll go far, though there is no sign of progress yet. Subordinative conjunctions are: that, if, unless, except, though, lest, because.

Interjections

These are independent of the construction of a sentence, and merely express an emotion of some kind: Bravo! Hurrah! Alas! Oh! Good gracious! Lo! Ah!

PRINCIPAL PREFIXES AND SUFFIXES

A PREFIX is something placed in front of a word to modify or extend its meaning. A suffix is something placed after a word for the same purpose.

Both prefixes and suffixes can be syllables, words, or merely single letters, as will be seen from the lists below.

Prefixes

a-. Has a considerable number of meanings: not (in *atheist, achromatic*); on (*ashore*); in (*asleep, abed*); out (*awake*); away (*arise*); from (*avert*); to (*ascend*); of (*athirst*).

ab-. From; off; away (as in *abdicate, absolve, abrogate, abstain, abrupt*). Note: In the word *abbreviate*, ab = ad.

ac-. A form of ad- when coming before *c* and *q* (as in *accuse, acquaint*); also a form of a- when used in *accurse*.

ad-. To (as in *adhere, adjust*). This prefix undergoes change before *b, c, f, g, l, n, p, q, r,* and *t*, becoming, variously, ab-, ac-, af-, ag-, al-, an-, ap-, ar-, as-, and at-. It is also abbreviated to a- before *sc,*

sp, st, and *gn* (as in *ascetic, asperse, astern,* and *agnostic*).

al-. All (as in *already, almost, alone*); also a form of ad- (*allocation*).

an-. A number of meanings: to (as in *annul*); up, back (*anode, analect*); on both sides (*ancillary*); not (*anarchy*).

ana-. Up, back, again (as in *anabaptism, anachronism*).

ante-. Before (as in *antedate, anteroom*).

anti-. Against; opposed to (as in *antipathy, anticlimax*—but in *anticipate*, the anti- is a corruption of ante-).

ap-. Forms of ad- and apo-, shortened to ap- before an aspirate (as in *aphorism*).

apo-. Off; from (as in *apology*).

arch-. Chief (as in *arch-deacon*).

auto-. Signifies action of, from, within, by or upon self (as in *automobile, autobiography*).

be-. By; near; on; about. This prefix has five distinct meanings: (1) It gives force to a word (as in *bedrug, befuddle, bedaub*); (2) It renders certain intransitive verbs transitive (*bemoan, bewail*); (3) It changes the meaning of certain transitive verbs (*beset, behold*); (4) It helps to form adverbs and prepositions (*before, behind*); (5) It forms verbs from nouns or adjectives (*befriend, belate*).

bi-. Two; twice (as in *bicycle, bichloride*). Is sometimes used as bin- (*binoculars*) and bis- (*biscuit*).

bio-. Life; having life (as in *biochemistry, biograph*).

cata-. Down; against; under (as in *catacomb, catastrophe*); and wholly (*catalogue*). It becomes cat- (*catarrh*) and cath- (*cathode*) before vowels.

centi-. Hundred (as in *centigrade, centimetre*).

centri-. Centre (as in *centrifugal, centripetal*).

chromo-. Colour; having colour (as in *chromolithograph, chromosphere*).

chrono-. Time (as in *chronograph, chronometer*).

circum-. About; around; on all sides (as in *circumference, circumnavigate*).

co-. Complementary to (as in *cosine*); together (*coact, coalition, co-operate*). Used as col- (*collate, collaborate*); com- (*combat, combine*); con- (*conclude, condition*); cor- (*correspond*).

contra-. Against; opposite to (as in *contradict, contraband*); also as contre- (*contretemps*) and contro- (*controvert*).

cosmo-. Order; the Universe (as in *cosmopolitan, cosmogony*).

counter-. Against, opposite to (as in *counteract, counterfeit*).

crypto-. Hidden (as in *cryptogram, cryptonym*).

cyclo-. Circle (as in *cyclometer, cyclorama*).

de-. From; of (as in *decadence, define*).

deca-. Ten (as in *decagon, decalogue*).

demi-. Half (as in *demigod, demiquaver*).

deutero-. Second (as in *deuterogamy*); also deuto- (*deutopiasm*).

dextro-. Towards the right (*dextrogyrate, dextroglucose*).

di-. Doubly, twofold (as in *dichromatic, dilemma*).

dia-. Through (as in *diagonal, diameter*); between (*diadem, dialect*).

dino-. Terrible (as in *dinosaur, dinotherium*).

dis-. Apart; asunder; a negative (as in *disagree, discard, discourage*).

e-. Out of; from—a shortened form of ex- which is used before consonants.

en-. In; into; to make (as in *enclave*, *endanger*). Also used as em- (*empale*).

epi-. Upon ; beside; over (as in *epidermis*, *epigram*).

es-. A form of ex- (in *escape*, *escheat*).

ex-. Out; out of; beyond (as in *exasperate*, *excite*). Also used in the forms e-, ec-, ef-, es-.

extra-. Outside; beyond (as in *extramural*, *extraordinary*).

for-. Thoroughly; greatly (as in *forlorn*); as a negative (*forbid*, *forget*).

fore-. Before (as in *forefather*, *foremast*).

gastro-. Stomach (as in *gastronomy*); also shortened to gastr- (*gastritis*).

geo-. Earth (as in *geography*, *geometry*).

hæmo-. See hemo-.

hecto-. A hundred (as in *hectolitre*, *hectograph*).

helio-. The sun (as in *heliograph*).

hemi-. Half (as in *hemisphere*).

hemo-. Blood (as in *hemorrhage*, *hemostatic*). Note: both hæmo- and hemo- are permissible forms.

hendeca-. Eleven (as in *hendecagon*).

hepta-. Seven (as in *heptagon*).

hetero-. Different (as in *heterodox*).

hexa-. Six (as in *hexagon*). Also as hex- (*hexangular*).

homo-. The same (as in *homogeneous*, *homologue*).

hydro-. Water (as in *hydroplane*, *hydrogen*); also as hydra- (*hydraulics*).

hygro-. Wet (as in *hygrometer*).

hyper-. Over; above (as in *hyperbole*, *hypercritical*).

hypo-. Under; beneath; less than (as in *hypophosphate*, *hypodermic*).

ichthyo-. A fish (as in *ichthyology*).

icos-. Twenty (as in *icosahedron*).

ideo-. Idea (as in *ideology*).

idio-. One's own (as in *idiosyncrasy*).

il-. A form of in- (found in *illogical*, *illegal*).

im-. A form of in- (found in *immature*).

in-. In; into; on (as in *incandescent*, *inhale*); not (as in *inattentive*, *insane*).

inter-. Between; together; among (as in *interact*, *interdependence*).

intra-. Within (as in *intramural*).

intro-. In; into; within (as in *introduction*, *intromit*).

iso-. Equal (as in *isosceles*, *isotope*).

kilo-. Thousand (as in *kilogram*, *kilowatt*).

kine-. Move (as in *kinematograph*, *kinetics*); now popularly spelt cine- in connection with motion pictures.

levo-. To the left (*levorotary*).

litho-. Stone (as in *lithography*).

Mac-. Son of (as in Scottish names).

mal-. Bad; ill-; wrong (as in *maladjust*, *malnutrition*, *malaria*).

mani-. A form of **manu-** (found in *manicure*).

manu-. Hand (as in *manufacture*, *manuscript*).

mega-. Large; a million (as in *megaphone*, *megadyne*).

meta-. Between (as in *metabolism*).

metro-. Measure (as in *metrology*); a mother (*metropolis*).

micro-. Small (as in *micrometer*, *microscope*).

mid-. Middle (as in *midday*, *midland*).

milli-. A thousand; a thousandth part (as in *millimetre*).

mis-. Wrong (as in *mistake*, *misdeal*, *misquote*).

mono-. Single; one (as in *monotype*, *monogamist*); also as **mon-** (*monad*, *monarch*).

multi-. Many (as in *multigraph*).

myri-. Numberless (as in *myriad*, *myriapod*).

neo-. New (as in *neolithic*, *neophyte*).

neuro-. Nerves (as in *neurologist*); also as **neur-** (*neuritis*, *neurasthenia*).

nitro-. Nitrogen (as in *nitrate*, *nitroglycerine*).

nom-. Name (as in *nominal*); also as **nomen-** (*nomenclature*).

non-. Not (as in *nondescript*, *nonplus*); also largely used hyphenated (*non-alcoholic*, *non-legal*).

ob-. Toward; over; upon; against (as in *object*, *oblique*, *obituary*, *obtrude*, *obtuse*).

oc-. A form of ob- before c (as in *occur*).

octa-. Eight (as in *octavo*); also as octo- (*octogenarian*).

oleo-. Oil (as in *oleograph*, *oleoresin*).

omni-. All (as in *omnibus*, *omnipotence*).

on-. At; by; with (as in *onward*, *onlooker*).

oo-. Egg (as in *oology*).

ortho-. Straight; direct; right (as in *orthodox*, *orthopedia*).

ossi-. Bone (as in *ossify*).

osteo-. Bone (as in *osteopath*).

out-. More than; beyond (as in *outbreak*, *outclass*, *outreach*). Also use in hyphen form (*out-fly*, *out-speak*).

over-. Too much (as in *overdraw*, *overcast*); also in the sense of *over* (*overcoat*); also in hyphen form (*overanxious*, *over-subscribe*).

oxy-. Sharp; acute; containing oxygen (as in *oxygen*, *oxygenic*); also as ox- (*oxide*).

pachy-. Thick (as in *pachyderm*).

paleo-. Ancient (as in *paleolithic*).

pan-. All (as in *panacea*, *panoply*); also used in hyphen form (*Pan-American*).

par-. A form of per- (as in *parboil*).

para-. Beside (as in *parallel*, *paramour*).

pedo-. Foot (as in *pedometer*).

penta-. Five (as in *pentagon, Pentateuch*).

per-. Through; by; by means of; for (as in *perceive, perjure, perennial, percentage*).

peri-. Near, around (as in *perimeter, period*).

petro-. Rock (as in *petroglyph*); also as petr- (*petroleum*).

photo-. Light (as in *photograph, photoelectric*).

pisci-. Fish (as in *pisciculture*); also as pisca- (*piscatory*).

poly-. Many; much (as in *polygamous, polygon*).

por-. A form of pro- (as in *portend*).

post-. Behind; after (as in *posthumous*); also in hyphen form (*post-graduate*).

pre-. Before (as in *preamble, preserve*).

pro-. Before; for; in favour of (as in *problem, procure*); also in hyphen form (*pro-Empire*).

proto-. First (as in *prototype, protocol*).

pseudo-. False (as in *pseudonym*); also used in hyphen form (*pseudo-satellite*).

psycho-. Soul (as in *psychology, psychopath*).

pyro-. Fire (as in *pyrometer*).

quadri-. Four (as in *quadrilateral*).

quasi-. Appearing as if—nearly always in hyphen form (as in *quasi-literature*).

re-. Back; backward; again (as in *return, readdress*).

retro-. Back; backward (as in *retrospect, retrograde*).

seismo-. Earthquake (as in *seismograph*).

self-. Same; identical (as in *selfishness, selfsame*); also used in hyphen form (*self-abasement*).

semi-. Half; partly (as in *semiquaver, semicircle*); also used in hyphen form (*semi-civilised*).

sexi-. Six—mostly used as sex- (as in *sexangle, sextant*).

step-. Relationship through marriage (as in *stepson*).

stereo-. Solid; hard (as in *stereoscope, stereotype*).

sub-. Under; from under (as in *subaltern, submarine*); also appears as suc-, suf-, sug-, sum-, sup-, sur-, subs-, sus-, or su- (*succeed, suffocate, suggest,* etc.); also used in hyphen form (*sub-agent, sub-lease*).

super-. Above; over (as in *superintend, supercargo*); also used in hyphen form (*super-ordinary*).

supra-. Above, beyond (as in *suprarenal*); also used in hyphen form (*supra-orbital*).

sur-. A form of super- (as in *surcoat, surface*).

sym-. A form of syn- (as in *symbol*).

syn-. With (as in *synchronous, syndicate*).

tetra. Four (as in *tetrahedron*).

tele-. Far off (as in *telegraph, telescope*).

theo-. A god (as in *theology*).

thermo-. Heat (as in *thermometer, thermostat*).

to-. To; towards (as in *together, toward*).

trans-. Across, beyond; through (as in *transact*); also as tran- (*transcribe*); also in hyphen form (*Trans-Siberian*).

tri-. Three; three times (as in *triangle, triennial*).

ultra-. Extreme (as in *ultramarine, ultraviolet*).

un-. Negation (as in *unabashed*); reversal (*unsaddle*).

under-. Beneath (as in *underline, understand*).

uni-. One (as in *uniform, unilateral*).

up-. Directed upwards (as in *uphill, upland*); also used in hyphen form (as in *upflow*).

vari-. Many (as in *variegated, variform*).

vice-. Substitute; subordinate (as in *viceroy*); also used in hyphen form (*vice-chancellor*); also used as vis- (*viscount*).

with-. Against (as in *withstand, without*).

zoo-. Animal (as in *zoological, zoometry*).

Suffixes

-able. Given to; tending to (as in *changeable, thinkable*).

-aceous. Of the nature of (as in *herbaceous*).

-acy. Forms nouns to denote a condition (as in *curacy, celibacy*).

-ad. Of (as in *Olympiad*)—usually preceded by *i*.

-ade. Of (as in *decade*).

-age. Forms collective nouns (as in *baggage, pilgrimage*).

-al. Of; like (as in *musical*).

-an. Pertaining to (as in *Lutheran*); sometimes with *i* (*Italian*).

-ana. Pertaining to (as in *Americana*); sometimes with *i* (*Dickensiana*).

-ance. Forming nouns from adjectives and verbs (as in *abundance, forbearance*).

-ane. Pertaining to (as in *humane*)—but note that, although this suffix has substantially the same meaning as -an, where both -an and -ane forms are known, there is a difference in meaning.

-ant. Forms nouns and adjectives of activity (as in *merchant, militant*).

-ar. Like; of (as in *regular, scholar*); also a form of -er (*beggar*).

-ard. Forms personal nouns (as in *drunkard, Savoyard*); also used as -art (*braggart*).

-arian. Forms adjectives and nouns (as in *vegetarian*).

-arium. Forms nouns denoting a place (as in *aquarium*); also used as -orium (*sanatorium*).

-ary. Makes nouns of persons and places (as in *voluptuary, library*); also adjectives (*secondary*).

-ate. Denotes function or condition (as in *magistrate, desolate*).

-atic. Of (as in *erratic*).

-ation. Forms nouns of action (as in *reformation, creation*).

-ator. Forms personal nouns of action (as in *arbitrator*).

-atory. Of (as in *exclamatory*).

-ble. Forms adjectives from verbs, usually preceded by a vowel—see -able.

-cide. Killer; destroyer (as in *germicide, fratricide*).

-cle. A diminutive (as in *particle*).

-cy. Denotes condition or quality (as in *aristocracy, magistracy*).

-dom. Indicates a quality (as in *martyrdom*).

-ed. Termination of the past tense and past participles of regular verbs (as in *educated, parted*).

-ee. Indicates a recipient (as in *payee, employee*); also used as a diminutive (*goatee*).

-en. Used (1) To form adjectives denoting material (as in *wheaten*); (2) To form verbs (*hasten*); (3) To form plurals of nouns (*oxen*).

-ent. Forms nouns indicating quality (as in *prudent*).

-er. Used (1) To form the comparative (as in *greater*); (2) To form nouns of performance (*beater*); (3) To form nouns of condition (*pensioner*).

-ery. Denotes business (as in *stationery, colliery*).

-es. Used to form certain plurals (as in *beeches, sexes*).

-ese. Forms adjectives and nouns from names of places (*Japanese, Genoese*).

-ess. Forms feminine nouns (as in *manageress*) and abstract nouns (*prowess*).

-est. Forms superlatives (as in *greatest*); also forms the second person singular (*lovest, goest*) following *thou*.

-ette. A feminine diminutive (as in *suffragette*).

-ferous. Producing; containing (as in *carboniferous*).

-fication. Making; rendering (as in *glorification*).

-fold. Denotes multiplication (as in *threefold, manifold*).

-form. Like; similar to (as in *cruciform*).

-ful. Full of (as in *bountiful*); also indicating a number of (*cupful, jugful*).

-fy. Making; to make (as in *solidify*).

-gram. Written; drawn (*telegram, parallelogram*).

-graph. That which writes; that which is written (as in *telegraph*).

-grapher. One who writes or produces graphically (as in *bibliographer, photographer*).

-graphy. Graphical description (as in *geography*).

-hood. Condition (as in *child-hood*).

-ic. Of, pertaining to (as in *scenic*, *nitric*).

-ics. Denoting a science (*physics*).

-ie. Makes a diminutive in names (as in *Julie*, *Rosie*).

-ier. Used in nouns denoting profession (as in *cashier*).

-in. Pertaining to (as in *lanolin*); frequently used as -ine (*gasoline*).

-ing. Used to form present participles (as in *skating*) and gerunds (*casting*).

-ior. Denotes a comparative degree (as in *superior*).

-ise. Denotes condition (as in *franchise*, *harmonise*).

-ish. In the nature of (as in *rakish*); also used to form adjectives from place-names (*English*, *Swedish*).

-ism. Denotes condition or doctrine (as in *hypnotism*, *pantheism*).

-ist. Denotes an agent or performer (as in *motorist*).

-ite. Of the nature of, like (as in *tripartite*).

-itis. An inflammation (as in *neuritis*).

-ive. Doing (as in *native*, *imperative*).

-ize. To make (as in *glamorize*, *mineralize*); frequently used in the form -ise.

-kin. A diminutive (as in *Peterkin*).

-less. A diminution of; without (as in *brainless*, *harmless*).

-let. A diminutive (as in *tablet*, *piglet*).

-like. Denoting similarity (as in *lifelike*).

-ling. A diminutive (as in *duckling*, *darling*).

-logy. Speech; spoken (as in *terminology*).

-ly. Like; in the nature of (as in *bravely*).

-lysis. Dissolving (as in *electrolysis*).

-ment. Used to form nouns denoting result or condition (as in *judgment*, *document*).

-meter. A measurer (as in *ammeter*, *galvanometer*).

-metry. The process of measuring (as in *geometry*).

-mony. Used to form nouns from other nouns (as in *patrimony*, *testimony*).

-most. Forms superlatives (as in *hindmost*).

-ness. Used to form abstract nouns (as in *happiness*, *darkness*).

-nomy. Denotes a science (as in *astronomy*).

-ock. A diminutive (as in *hillock*).

-ode. Direction (as in *anode*, *episode*).

-oid. Resembling (as in *celluloid*).

-ol. Denoting (specifically) an alcohol or an oil (as in *phenol*, *petrol*).

-ology. Denoting a science (as in *philology*) or a collection (*anthology*).

-or. Denotes an agent (as in *actor*, *prosecutor*) and forms abstract nouns (*terror*).

-osity. An abundance of (as in *curiosity*).

-ot. A diminutive (as in *ballot*); also indicates origin (*Cypriot*).

-ous. Denotes possession of a quality (as in *vigorous*).

-path. A treater of disease (as in *nueropath*).

-pathy. The treatment of disease (as in *homeopathy*).

-phile. Loving (as in *bibliophile*).

-phobe. Being averse to (as in *Anglophobe*).

-phobia. Horror; dread (as in *claustrophobia*).

-phone. A sound (as in *telephone*).

-ple. Used to form multiplicatives (as in *quadruple*).

-ric. Indicates jurisdiction (as in *bishopric*).

-scope. An indicator (as in *microscope*).

-ship. Denotes a condition or office (as in *friendship*, *professorship*).

-some. Used to form adjectives denoting quality (as in *quarrelsome*).

-son. In names, the son of (as in *Jackson*).

-ster. Denotes a profession, occupation or state (as *seamster*, *spinster*, *youngster*).

-stress. The feminine of -ster.

-th. Used in: (1) abstract nouns (as in *health*); (2) ordinal numbers (*twelfth*); and (3) the third person singular of the present indicative (*hath*).

-tion. Forms nouns of action (as in *temptation*).

-tious. Forms adjectives of nouns ending in -tion.

-tome. An agency for cutting as (in *microtome*).

-tomy. The act of cutting (as in *appendicectomy*).

-ton. In place names, a town (as *Bridgton*).

-tor. See -or.

-trix. The feminine ending of nouns of profession ending in -tor (as in *prosecutrix*).

-trope. Indicates turning (as in *heliotrope*).

-trophy. Nutrition (as in *atrophy*).

-tude. Indicates being (as in *gratitude*).

-ty. Ten (as in *fifty*); and a termination of abstract nouns (*nullity*).

-ule. A diminutive (as in *granule*).

-ulous. Full of (as in *credulous*).

-ure. Indicates action (as in *seizure*).

-ute. Forms adjectives and verbs (as in *absolute*, *constitute*).

-ways. Indicates a direction (as in *longways*, *always*).

-wise. Indicates a manner (as *contrariwise*).

-worth. Used to indicate worthy (as in *pennyworth*).

-y. Forms diminutive (as in *Johnny*); indicates a quality in adjectives (as in *lazy*, *rainy*).

COMMON ABBREVIATIONS

This list contains many of the abbreviations usually found in books and reading matter generally, as well as short forms of degrees, professional qualifications, and titles.

a. *annus* (year), *ante* (before).

A.1 First class.

A.A. Automobile Association.

A.A.A. Amateur Athletic Association.

A.B. *Artium Baccalaureus* (Bachelor of Arts), able-bodied seaman.

abbr., abbrev. Abbreviated, abbreviation.

A.C. Alternating current.

A.C.A. Associate of the Institute of Chartered Accountants.

A.C.I.I. Associate of the Chartered Insurance Institute.

A.C.I.S. Associate of the Chartered Institute of Secretaries.

A.D. *Anno Domini* (in the year of our Lord).

A.D.C. Aide-de-camp.

ad inf. *Ad infinitum* (to infinity).

ad int. *Ad interim* (in the meantime).

Adj. Adjutant.

ad lib. *Ad libitum* (at pleasure).

ad val. *Ad valorem* (according to the value).

A.E.A. Atomic Energy Authority.

A.F.C. Air Force Cross.

Agr.B. *Agriculturæ Baccalaureus* (Bachelor of Agriculture).

A.I.A. Associate of the Institute of Actuaries.

A.I.C.S. Associate of the Institute of Chartered Shipbrokers.

A.Inst.P. Associate of Institute of Physics.

A.K.C. Associate of King's College, London.

A.M. *Anno Mundi* (in the year of the world), *ante meridiem* (before noon), *Artium Magister* (Master of Arts).

A.M.I.C.E. Associate Member of the Institute of Civil Engineers.

A.M.I.E.E. Associate Member of the Institute of Electrical Engineers.

A.M.I.Mech.E. Associate Member of the Institute of Mechanical Engineers.

amp. Ampere.

Ang.-Sax. Anglo-Saxon.

Anon. Anonymous.

Anzac. Australian and New Zealand Army Corps.

A.P.S. Associate of the Pharmaceutical Society.

aq. *Aqua* (water).

A.R.A. Associate of the Royal Academy.

A.R.A.M. Associate of the Royal Academy of Music.

A.R.C.M. Associate of the Royal College of Music.

A.R.C.O. Associate of the Royal College of Organists.

A.R.I.B.A. Associate Royal Institute of British Architects.

A.R.S.A. Associate of the Royal Scottish Academy, Associate of the Royal Society of Arts.

A.R.S.L. Associate of the Royal Society of Literature.

A.R.S.M. Associate of the Royal School of Mines.

A.R.W.S. Associate of Royal Water-colour Society.

A.S. Academy of Science.

A.S.A. Atomic Scientists' Association.

ASDIC. Anti-Submarine Detector Indicator Committee.

A.T.A. Air Transport Auxiliary.

A.T.C. Air Training Corps.

aux., auxil. Auxiliary.

B.A. Bachelor of Arts, British Association (for the Advancement of Science).

B.Agr. = Agr.B. Bachelor of Agriculture.

Ball. Balliol College, Oxford.

B.A.O.R. British Army of the Rhine.

Bart., Bt. Baronet.

Bart's. St. Bartholomew's Hospital, London.

B.B.C. British Broadcasting Corporation.

B.C. Before Christ, British Columbia.

B.Ch. Bachelor of Surgery.

B.C.L. Bachelor of Civil Law.

B.D. Bachelor of Divinity.

B.D.S. Bachelor of Dental Surgery.

B.E., B.Eng. Bachelor of Engineering.

B.L. Bachelor of Laws.

B.Litt. Bachelor of Literature.

B.M. Bachelor of Medicine, Bench-Mark (surveying).

B.M.A. British Medical Association.

B.Mus. Bachelor of Music.

B.N.C. Brasenose College, Oxford.

B.O.A.C. British Overseas Airways Corporation.

B.O.T. Board of Trade.

B.O.T.U. Board of Trade Unit = 1 kilowatt-hour.

B.P. British Pharmacopeia.

Brig. Brigade, Brigadier.

Brit. Britain, Britannia, British.

Brit. Mus. British Museum.

B.S. Bachelor of Surgery.

B.Sc. Bachelor of Science.

B.S.T. British Summer Time.

B.Th.U. British Thermal Unit.

Bt. Baronet.

B.W.I. British West Indies.

C. Cape, Centigrade, Conservative. — **c.** Caught (cricket), cent, centime, centimetre, centum.

C.A. Chartered Accountant.

Cai. Gonville and Caius College, Cambridge.

cap. (caps., pl.). Capital letter, *caput* (chapter), number of an Act of Parliament.

C.B. Companion of the Bath.

C.B.E. Commander of Order of British Empire.

C.C. Caius College, Cambridge.—**c.c.** Cubic centimetre.

C.C.C. Christ's College (Cambridge), Corpus Christi College (Oxford or Cambridge).

C.C.G. Control Commission, Germany.

C.D. Civil Defence.

C.D.H. College Diploma in Horticulture.

cen. Century.

C.G. Coastguard, Consul-General.

C.G.M. Conspicuous Gallantry Medal.

C.H. Companion of Honour.

C.I. Imperial Order of the Crown of India (for ladies), Channel Islands.

C.I.D. Criminal Investigation Department.

C.I.E. Companion of the Order of the Indian Empire.

C.I.G.S. Chief of Imperial General Staff.

C.I.O. Committee for Industrial Organisation.

cir., circ. *Circa, circiter, circum* (about).

C.J. Chief Justice.

C.M. Master of Surgery.

cmd. Command paper (Govt. publication).

C.M.G. Companion of the Order of St. Michael and St. George.

C.O. Commanding Officer, Combined Operations.—**c.o.** Care of.

Co. Company, County.

C.O.D. Cash on delivery.

C. of E. Church of England.

C.O.I. Central Office of Information

Col. Colonel.—**col.** College, column.

Comdt. Commandant.

Consol. Consolidated.

cos. Cosine.

cosec. Cosecant.

cot. Cotangent.

Cpl. Corporal.

C.P.R. Canadian Pacific Railway.

Cr. Credit, creditor.

cres. *Crescendo* (increasing).

C.R.O. Criminal Record Office.

cryst. Crystallised.

C.S.I. Companion of the Order of the Star of India.

C.T. Certificated Teacher.

C.T.C. Cyclist Touring Club.

Cu., cub. Cubic.

C.U.B.C. Cambridge University Boat Club.

C.U.D.S. Cambridge University Dramatic Society.

C.V.O. Commander of the Royal Victorian Order.

c.w.o. Cash with order.

cwt. Hundredweight.

D. *Dominus* (Lord).—**d.** daughter, *denarius* or *denarii* (penny, pence), died.

D.B.E. Dame of the British Empire.

D.C. *Da capo* (from the beginning), District Commissioner, District of Columbia, direct current.

D.C.L. Doctor of Civil Law.

D.C.M. Distinguished Conduct Medal.

D.C.V.O. Dame Commander of the Royal Victorian Order.

D.D. Doctor of Divinity.

D.D.S. Doctor of Dental Surgery

D.D.T. Dichlorodiphenyl-trichloroethane.

D.Eng. Doctor of Engineering.

D.F. Defender of the Faith.

D.F.C. Distinguished Flying Cross.

D.G. *Dei gratia* (by the grace of God), Director-General.

D.Hy. Doctor of Hygiene.

D.L. Deputy Lieutenant.

D.Litt., D.L. Doctor of Literature.

D.L.O. Dead Letter Office.

D.Mus. Doctor of Music.

D.N.B. Dictionary of National Biography.

do. Ditto.

dol. (dols., pl.). Dollar.

doz. Dozen.

D.P. Displaced Person.

D.Phil. Doctor of Philosophy.

D.P.O. District Post-office.

D.R. Dead reckoning.

Dr. Debtor, doctor.

Dram. Pers. *Dramatis personæ* (the persons of the drama).

D.S. *Dal segno* (from the sign), Dental Surgeon.

D.S.C. Distinguished Service Cross.

D.Sc. Doctor of Science.

D.S.M. Distinguished Service Medal.

D.S.O. Distinguished Service Order.

D.T., D.Th. Doctor of Theology.

D.V. *Deo volente* (God being willing).

D.V.S. Doctor of Veterinary Science.

dwt. A pennyweight.

E. East.

ea. Each.

E.A.M.S. East African Medical Service.

E. and F.C. Examined and found correct.

E. and O.E. Errors and omissions excepted.

e.g. *Exempli gratia* (for the sake of example).

Emm. Emmanuel College, Cambridge.

E.P.U. European Payments Union.

E.P.N.S. Electro-plated nickel silver.

eq. Equal.—**equiv.** Equivalent.

E.R.P. European Recovery Plan.

Esq. Esquire.

et al. *Et alibi* (and elsewhere), *et alii* or *aliæ* (and others).

etc., &c. *Et cetera* (and the rest).

Exam. Examination.

Exc. Excellency.

F. Fahrenheit, Fellow, Friday.—**f.** Fathom, feminine, forte, franc.

F.A. Football Association.

Fah., Fahr. Fahrenheit.

F.A.I. Fellow of the Auctioneers Institute.

F.A.N.Y. First Aid Nursing Yeomanry.

F.A.O. Food and Agriculture Organisation.

F.B.A. Fellow of the British Academy.

F.B.I. Federation of British Industries; Federal Bureau of Investigation (in U.S.A.).

F.C.A. Fellow of the Institute of Chartered Accountants.

F.C.I.I. Fellow of the Chartered Insurance Institute.

F.C.P. Fellow of the College of Preceptors.

F.C.P.S. Fellow of the Cambridge Philosophical Society.

F.C.S. Fellow of the Chemical Society.

F.D. *Fidei Defensor* (Defender of the Faith).

fem. Feminine.

F.G.S. Fellow of the Geological Society.

F.I.A. Fellow of the Institute of Actuaries.

F.I.C. Fellow of the Chemical Institute.

Fid. Def. Defender of the Faith.

F.I.D.O. Fog Investigation and Dispersal Operation.

F.I.Inst. Fellow of the Imperial Institute.

F.Inst.P. Fellow of the Institute of Physics.

F.M. Field-Marshal, Frequency Modulation.

F.O. Foreign Office.

f.o.b. Free on board, i.e., price not including sea-carriage.

f.o.r. Free on rail, i.e., price not including land-carriage.

F.P.S. Fellow of the Pharmaceutical Society.

Fr. French.—**fr.** Franc.

F.R.A.M. Fellow of the Royal Academy of Music.

F.R.A.S. Fellow of the Royal Astronomical Society.

F.R.B.S. Fellow of the Royal Botanical Society.

F.R.C.I. Fellow of the Royal Colonial Institute.

F.R.C.M. Fellow of the Royal College of Music.

F.R.C.O. Fellow of the Royal College of Organists.

F.R.C.P. Fellow of the Royal College of Physicians.

F.R.C.S. Fellow of the Royal College of Surgeons.

F.R.C.V.S. Fellow of the Royal College of Veterinary Surgeons.

F.R.G.S. Fellow of the Royal Geographical Society.

F.R.H.S. Fellow of the Royal Horticultural Society.

F.R.Hist.S. Fellow of the Royal Historical Society.

F.R.I.B.A. Fellow of the Royal Institute of British Architects.

F.R.M.S. Fellow of the Royal Microscopical Society.

F.R.Met.S. Fellow of the Royal Meteorological Society.

F.R.S. *Fraternitatis Regiæ Socius* (Fellow of the Royal Society).

F.R.S.E. Fellow of the Royal Society of Edinburgh.

F.R.S.L. Fellow of the Royal Society of Literature.

F.R.S.S. Fellow of the Royal Statistical Society.

F.S.A. Fellow of the Society of Antiquaries, Fellow of the Society of Arts.

F.S.I. Fellow of the Surveyors' Institution.

F.S.S. Fellow of the Statistical Society.

F.T.C.D. Fellow of Trinity College, Dublin.

F.Z.S. Fellow of the Zoological Society.

G. Gulf.
G.A.T.T. General Agreement on Tariffs and Trade.
G.B. Great Britain.
G.B. & I. Great Britain and Ireland.
G.B.E. Knight or Dame Grand Cross of the Order of the British Empire.
G.C. George Cross.
G.C.B. Grand Cross of the Order of the Bath.
g.c.d. or **m.** Greatest common divisor, or measure.
G.C.I.E. Grand Commander of the Indian Empire.
G.C.L.H. Grand Commander of the Legion of Honour.
G.C.M.G. Grand Cross of the Order of St. Michael and St. George.
G.C.S.I. Grand Commander of the Order of the Star of India.
G.C.V.O. Grand Commander of the Royal Victorian Order.
G.H.Q. General Headquarters.
G.M. George Medal.
G.M.K.P. Grand Master of the Knights of St. Patrick.
G.M.S.I. Grand Master of the Star of India.
G.M.T. Greenwich Mean Time.
G.O.C. General Officer Commanding.
G.P. General Practitioner.
G.P.O. General Post Office.
G.P.U. *Gosudarstvenoe politicheskoe upravlenie* (State Political Department).

G.R.C.M. Graduate of the Royal College of Music.
G.R.I. *Georgius Rex et Imperator* (George King and Emperor).

H.A.C. Honourable Artillery Company.
H.E. His Excellency.—**h.e.** *Hic est* (this is), *hoc est* (that is).
H.H. His (or Her) Highness.
H.L.I. Highland Light Infantry.
H.M. His (or Her) Majesty.
H.M.S. Her Majesty's Ship (or Service).
H.M.S.O. Her Majesty's Stationery Office.
Hon. Honourable, honorary.
H.P. Horse-power.
H.Q. Head-quarters.
H.R.H. His (or Her) Royal Highness.
hund. Hundred.

I.C.A.O. International Civil Aviation Organisation.
I.C.E. Institute of Civil Engineers.
i.e. *Id est* (that is).
I.L.O. International Labour Organisation.
I.M.C.O. International Maritime Consultative Organisation.
Inc. Incorporated.
inst. Instant (current month).
Inst. Act. Institute of Actuaries.
I.O.M. Isle of Man.
I.O.U. I owe you.
I.Q. Intelligence Quotient.
I.R.O. International Refugee Organisation.
I.S.O. Imperial Service Order.

I.T.A. Independent Television Authority.
I.T.O. International Trade Organisation.
I.T.U. International Telecommunication Union.
I.W. Isle of Wight.

J. (JJ., pl.). Judge, Justice.
J.A.G. Judge Advocate-General.
J.D. *Jurum Doctor* (Doctor of Laws).
J.P. Justice of the Peace.

K.B. Knight Bachelor.
K.B.E. Knight of the Order of the British Empire.
K.C.B. Knight Commander of the Bath.
K.C.I.E. Knight Commander of the Indian Empire.
K.C.M.G. Knight Commander of the Order of St. Michael and St. George.
K.C.S.I. Knight Commander of the Star of India.
K.C.V.O. Knight Commander of the Royal Victorian Order.
K.G. Knight of the Garter.
K.P. Knight of the Order of St. Patrick.
K.T. Knight of the Order of the Thistle.
Kt. Knight.

L.A. Literate in Arts.
L.A.C. Licentiate of the Apothecaries' Company.
l.b.w. Leg before wicket (cricket).
L.C.C. London County Council.
L.C.J. Lord Chief Justice.

l.c.m. Least common multiple.
L.C.P. Licentiate of the College of Preceptors.
L.D.S. Licentiate in Dental Surgery.
Lib. Liberal.
Litt.D. Doctor of Literature.
L.J. Lord Justice.
LL.B. Bachelor of Laws.
LL.D. Doctor of Laws.
LL.M. Master of Laws.
L.N.U. League of Nations Union.
L.P.S. Lord Privy Seal.
L.P.T.B. London Passenger Transport Board.
L.R.A.M. Licentiate of the Royal Academy of Music.
L.R.C.P. Licentiate of the Royal College of Physicians.
L.R.C.S. Licentiate of the Royal College of Surgeons.
L.R.C.V.S. Licentiate of the Royal College of Veterinary Surgeons.
L.S.A. Licentiate of the Society of Apothecaries.
L.T.A. Lawn Tennis Association.
Ltd., Ld. Limited.

M. *Mille* (one thousand), Monday, Monsieur.—**m.** Married, masculine, *meridiem* (noon), minute, month.
M.A. Master of Arts, Military Academy.
mas., masc. Masculine.
M.B. *Medicinæ baccalaureus*, Bachelor of Medicine.
M.B.E. Member of the British Empire.
M.C. Military Cross, Master of Ceremonies.

M.C.C. Marylebone Cricket Club.

M.Ch. Master of Surgery.

M.C.P. Member of the College of Preceptors.

M.C.P.S. Member of the Cambridge Philosophical Society.

M.D. *Medicinæ Doctor*, Doctor of Medicine.

mdlle. Mademoiselle.

Mem., Memo. Memorandum.

Messrs., MM. *Messieurs* (gentlemen).

M.F.H. Master of the Foxhounds.

Mgr. Monseigneur.

M.H.R. Member of the House of Representatives (Colonial and U.S.).

M.I.C.E. Member of the Institute of Civil Engineers.

M.I.E.E. Member of the Institute of Electrical Engineers.

M.I.M.E. Member of the Institute of Mining Engineers.

M.I.Mech.E. Member of the Institute of Mechanical Engineers.

min. Minute.

Mlle. Mademoiselle.

M.M. Messrs., Military Medal.

Mme. (Mmes., pl.). Madame.

M.O. Medical Officer, Money order.

Mods. Moderations (at Oxford).

M.O.H. Medical Officer of Health.

Mons. Monsieur. — **Monsig.** Monsignor.

M.O.W. Ministry of Works.

M.P. Member of Parliament, Military Police.

m.p.h. Miles per hour.

M.P.S. Member of the Pharmaceutical Society.

M.R. Master of the Rolls.

M.R.A.C. Member of the Royal Agricultural College.

M.R.A.M. Member of the Royal Academy of Music.

M.R.A.S. Member of the Royal Astronomical Society, also Royal Asiatic Society.

M.R.C.P. Member of the Royal College of Physicians.

M.R.C.S. Member of the Royal College of Surgeons.

M.R.C.V.S. Member of the Royal College of Veterinary Surgeons.

M.R.G.S. Member of the Royal Geographical Society.

M.R.I. Member of the Royal Institution.

M.R.I.B.A. Member of the Royal Institute of British Architects.

M.R.I.E.E. Member of the Royal Institute of Electrical Engineers.

M.R.S.L. Member of the Royal Society of Literature.

M.S. Master in Surgery.

MS. (MSS., pl.). Manuscript.

M.S.A. Member of the Society of Architects.

Mus.B., Mus.Bac. Bachelor of Music.

Mus.D. Doctor of Music.

M.V.O. Member of the Royal Victorian Order.

M.W.B. Metropolitan Water Board.

N.A.A.F.I. Navy, Army, and Air Force Institutes.

N.B. New Brunswick, North Britain, North British, *nota bene* (note well).

N.C.B. National Coal Board.

N.C.O. Non-commisioned officer.

N.E.C. National Executive Committee.

nem. con. *Nemine contradicente* (no one opposing, unanimously).

N.H.S. National Health Service.

N.I. National Insurance, Northern Ireland.

N.L. National Liberal.

Non. con. Not content (the term used in voting in the House of Lords).

non seq. *Non sequitur* (it does not follow).

N.S.P.C.C. National Society for the Prevention of Cruelty to Children.

N.S.W. New South Wales.

N.U.S. National Union of Students.

N.U.T. National Union of Teachers.

N.Y. New York (U.S.).

N.Z. New Zealand.

O.B.E. Officer of the Order of the British Empire.

O.C. Officer-in-Command.

O.C.T.U. Officer Cadet Training Unit.

O.E.E.C. Organisation for European Economic Co-operation.

O.H.M.S. On Her Majesty's Service.

O.M. Order of Merit.

Or. Oriel College (Oxford).

O.T.C. Officers' Training Corps.

O.U.B.C. Oxford University Boat Club.

O.U.D.S. Oxford University Dramatic Society.

Oxf. Oxford.—**Oxon.** *Oxonia* (Oxford), *Oxoniensis* (of Oxford).

P. & O. Peninsular and Oriental Steam Navigation Co.

par. Paragraph, parallel.

P.A.Y.E. Pay As You Earn.

P.C. Privy Councillor, Police constable.

Ph.B. Bachelor of Philosophy.

Ph.D. Doctor of Philosophy.

phot., photog. Photographic, photography.

P.L.A. Port of London Authority.

P.M. Prime Minister, Provost-Marshal, *post meridiem* (afternoon).

P.M.G. Postmaster-General, Paymaster-General.

P.M.O. Principal Medical Officer.

P.N.E.U. Parents' National Educational Union.

P.O. Post-office, Postal order.

P.O.S.B. Post Office Savings Bank.

P.P. *Per procurationem*, i.e., on behalf of, as agent for.

P.P.C. *Pour prendre congé* (to take leave).

P.R. Proportional Representation.

P.R.A. President of the Royal Academy.

P.R.I.B.A. President of the Royal Institute of British Architects.

Prof. Professor.

pro tem. *Pro tempore* (for the time being).

prox. *Proximo* (next month).

P.R.S. President of the Royal Society.

P.R.S.A. President of the Royal Scottish Academy.

P.R.S.E. President of the Royal Society, Edinburgh.

P.S. *Post scriptum* (P.P.S., pl.), written afterwards.

P.T. Physical Training.

Pt. Port.

P.T.O. Please turn over.

Q.B.D. Queen's Bench Division.

Q.C. Queen's Counsel.

q.e. *Quod est* (which is).

q.e.d. *Quod erat demonstrandum* (which was to be demonstrated).

q.e.f. *Quod erat faciendum* (which was to be done).

Q.M. Quartermaster.—

Q.M.G. Quartermaster-General.

Q.V. *Quantum vis* (as much as you wish).—**q.v.** *Quod vide* (which see).

Qy. Query.

R. Railway, Réaumur, Republican, river.

R.A. Royal Academy, Royal Regiment of Artillery.

R.A.C. Royal Armoured Corps, Royal Automobile Club.

R.A.D.A. Royal Academy of Dramatic Art.

R.A.E.C. Royal Army Education Corps.

R.A.F. Royal Air Force.

R.A.M. Royal Academy of Music.

R.A.M.C. Royal Army Medical Corps.

R.A.O.C. Royal Army Ordnance Corps.

R.A.P.C. Royal Army Pay Corps.

R.A.S.C. Royal Army Service Corps.

R.A.S.E. Royal Agricultural Society of England.

R.A.V.C. Royal Army Veterinary Corps.

R.B.A. Royal Society of British Artists.

R.C. Roman Catholic.

R.C.M. Royal College of Music.

R.C.P. Royal College of Preceptors, Royal College of Physicians.

R.C.S. Royal College of Surgeons.

R.D. Refer to drawer (formula on a cheque returned by bankers unpaid to payee).

R.D.C. Rural District Council.

R.E. Royal Engineers.

R.E.M.E. Royal Electrical and Mechanical Engineers.

Rev. (Revs., pl.). Reverend.

R.F. *République française* (French Republic).

R.F.A. Royal Field Artillery.

R.G.A. Royal Garrison Artillery.

R.G.S. Royal Geographical Society.

R.H. Royal Highness.

R.H.A. Royal Horse Artillery, Royal Hibernian Academy.

R.H.S. Royal Humane Society.

R.I.B.A. Royal Institute of British Architects.

R.I.P. *Requiescat in pace* (may he [or she] rest in peace).

R.M.A. Royal Military Academy, Woolwich, Royal Marine Artillery.

R.M.C. Royal Military College, Sandhurst.

R.M.L.I. Royal Marine Light Infantry.

R.M.S. Royal Mail Steamer.

R.N. Royal Navy.

R.N.C. Royal Naval College.

R.N.L.I. Royal National Lifeboat Institution.

R.N.R. Royal Naval Reserve.

R.N.V.R. Royal Naval Volunteer Reserve.

R.O.C. Royal Observer Corps.

R.P. Reply paid.

r.p.m. Revolutions per minute.

R.R. Railroad, Right Reverend.

R.R.C. Royal Red Cross.

R.S. Royal Society, Revised Statutes.

Rs. Rupees.

R.S.A. Royal Scottish Academy, Royal Society of Arts.

R.S.D. Royal Society, Dublin.

R.S.E. Royal Society, Edinburgh.

R.S.F.S.R. Russian Soviet Federated Socialist Republic.

R.S.M. Royal School of Mines, Regimental Sergeant-Major.

R.S.O. Railway Sorting Office.

R.S.P.C.A. Royal Society for the Prevention of Cruelty to Animals.

R.S.S. *Regiæ Societatis Socius* (Fellow of the Royal Society).

R.S.V.P. *Répondez, s'il vous plaît* (answer, if you please).

R.T.F. *Radiodiffusion et Télévision Française* (French Broadcasting and Television service).

Rt. Hon. Right Honourable.

Rt. Rev. Right Reverend.

R.U. Rugby Union.

R.V.C. Royal Veterinary College.

R.W.S. Royal Society of Painters in Water Colours.

R.Y.S. Royal Yacht Squadron.

S. Saint.

Sc.D. Doctor of Science.

Sec. Secant, second.

Sen. Senior.

sin. *Sine.*—**sing.** Singular.

S.M. Sergeant-Major.

Soc. Society.

S.O.S. Save our souls: the signal for help from a sinking ship.

sp. gr. Specific gravity.

S.P.Q.R. *Senatus Populusque Romanus* (the Roman Senate and People).

S.R.N. State Registered Nurse.

S.R.S. *Societatis Regiæ Socius* (Fellow of the Royal Society).

S.S. Steamship.

St. Saint, strait, street.

ster. Sterling.

stet. Let it remain.

Supt. Superintendent.

Surg. Surgeon.

S.W. South-west, -ern.

T.A. Territorial Army.

tan. Tangent.

T.B. Tuberculosis.

T.D. Territorial Decoration.

T.H. Their Highnesses.

T.H.W.M. Trinity High Water Mark.

tinct. Tincture.

T.M. Their Majesties.

T.N.T. Trinitrotoluol.

T.O. Telegraph office, turn over.

T.R.H. Their Royal Highnesses.

T.T. Tuberculin tested.

T.U.C. Trades Union Congress.

T.V.A. Tennessee Valley Authority.

U.S.I. United Service Institution.

U.D.C. Urban District Council.

U.K. United Kingdom.

ult. *Ultimo* (last month).

U.N. United Nations.

U.N.A. United Nations Association.

U.N.E.S.C.O. United Nations Educational, Scientific, and Cultural Organisation.

ung. *Unguentum* (ointment).

U.N.I.C.E.F. United Nations International Children's Emergency Fund.

U.P.U. Universal Postal Union.

U.S. United States.

U.S.A. United States of America.

U.S.S.R. Union of the Soviet Socialist Republics.

v. Verb, *versus* (against), *vide* (see).

V.A.D. Voluntary Aid Detachment.

V.C. Victoria Cross.

verb sap. *Verbum sapientis satis* (a word to the wise is enough).

vid. *Vide* (see).

V.I.P. Very Important Person.

viz. *Videlicet* (to wit, namely).

vol. (vols., pl.). Volume.

vs. *Versus* (against).

W.D. War Department.

W.H.O. World Health Organisation.

W.O. War Office, warrant officer.

W.R.A.C. Women's Royal Auxiliary Corps.

W.R.A.F. Women's Royal Air Force.

W.R.N.S. Women's Royal Naval Service.

W.S. Writer to the Signet.

wt. Weight.

W.V.S. Women's Voluntary Services.

Xmas. Christmas.

yd. (yds., pl.). Yard.

Y.M.C.A. Young Men's Christian Association.

Y.W.C.A. Young Women's Christian Association.

COMMON FOREIGN PHRASES

ENGLISH-SPEAKING people often say and write words or
phrases in foreign languages because there is no equivalent in English which will give them the exact shade of meaning they want. Some of those words and phrases are as
familiar as English itself.

Below are just a few of those most frequently used. Their
origins are marked thus: Fr.=French; Ger.=German;
Gr.=Greek; It.=Italian; L.=Latin; Sp.=Spanish.

A

à bon droit (Fr.): With good right.
à compte (Fr.): On account; in part payment.
à fond (Fr.): Completely.
a fortiori (L.): With stronger reason.
à la bonne heure (Fr.): At the lucky moment.
à la carte (Fr.): According to the bill of fare (said of a meal
    when dishes are ordered individually—see **table d'hôte**).
à la française (Fr.): In the French manner.
à la mode (Fr.): In fashion.
a posteriori (L.): From the latter; from the effect to the cause.
a priori (L.): From the former; from the cause to the effect.
à votre santé (Fr.): Good health! (often abbreviated to **santé**).
à vuestra salud (Sp.): Good health! (often abbreviated to
    salud).
ab initio (L.): From the beginning.
ad hoc (L.): For this special purpose.
ad infinitum (L.): To infinity; for ever.
ad interim (L.): In the meanwhile; temporarily.
ad libitum (L.): At pleasure; to any extent (often shortened
    to **ad lib.**).
ad nauseam (L.): To the point of disgust.
ad valorem (L.): According to value (**ad valorem duty** is duty
    paid on value and not on weight).
adsum (L.): I am present (used in some schools at roll-call).
affaire d'honneur (Fr.): An affair of honour; a duel.

agent provocateur (Fr.): A person employed to provoke some-one into doing some wrongful act (literally, a provoking agent).

alter ego (L.): Another self.

amah (Portuguese and Anglo-Indian): A servant who looks after children; a native nurse.

amende honorable (Fr.): An apology; reparation.

amour-propre (Fr.): Self-esteem.

ante meridiem (L.): Before noon (nearly always shortened to a.m.).

au contraire (Fr.): On the contrary.

au courant (Fr.): Fully acquainted (with the circumstances).

au fond (Fr.): At bottom; fundamentally

au naturel (Fr.): In a natural state (used in cooking to denote "without garnishing").

au pair (Fr.): On mutual terms (used to denote an exchange of services without any money changing hands).

auf wiedersehen (Ger.): To our next meeting.

au revoir (Fr.): To our next meeting.

B

bitte (Ger.): If you please.

bon marché (Fr.): A bargain; a cheap bazaar.

bon vivant (Fr.): A gourmet; one who likes much good food.

bon voyage! (Fr.): A good journey to you!

bouillabaisse (Fr.): A fish soup flavoured with garlic (a favourite dish in the south of France).

C

canaille (Fr.): Rabble; common people.

casus belli (L.): A cause of war.

cause célèbre (Fr.): A famous trial or lawsuit.

caveat emptor (L.): Let the buyer beware (meaning that it is up to buyer to make sure he is getting value for money).

chemin de fer (Fr.): Railway; also a game of cards.

cherchez la femme (Fr.): Look for the woman (meaning that behind the circumstances there will be found a woman).

chevalier d'industrie (Fr.): A swindler; an adventurer.

ci-devant (Fr.): Formerly; once was.

comme il faut (Fr.): In good taste; acceptable.

compos mentis (L.): In possession of one's faculties; all there; the reverse of stupid.

corps de ballet (Fr.): The dancers in a ballet.

corps d'élite (Fr.): A body of picked men.

corps diplomatique (Fr.): The body of diplomatists in a capital.

coup de maître (Fr.): A master-stroke.

coup d'essai (Fr.): A first attempt.

crème de la crème (Fr.): The cream of the cream; perfection.

cui bono? (L.): For whose benefit (used to mean "What good will it do?").

cum grano salis (L.): With a grain of salt; with reservations; with lack of complete belief.

D

d'accord (Fr.): In accord; agreed.

de facto (L.): In fact; reality.

de jure (L.): By right of law.

de luxe (Fr.): Of special quality; luxurious.

de novo (L.): Anew; afresh.

de rigueur (Fr.): Necessary; not to be dispensed with.

de trop (Fr.): In the way; not wanted.

dernier cri (Fr.): The latest fashion.

deus ex machinâ (L.): A god from the machine (used to denote how a situation has been saved when everything looked hopeless; an eleventh-hour solution).

Dieu et mon droit (Fr.): God and my right (the motto of British kings).

double entente (Fr.): Double meaning (often written **double entendre**, which is incorrect).

E

editio princeps (L.): First edition.

édition de luxe (Fr.): a finely printed and bound edition.

embarras de richesse (Fr.): Difficulty caused by having very much money, or too much of something considered to be good.

en casserole (Fr.) Cooked in a saucepan with vegetables.

en clair (Fr.): In clear; not in cipher; in plain language.

en déshabillé (Fr.): In undress; in clothes suitable for lounging or resting.

en famille (Fr.): In the family; informal; pot-luck.
en fête (Fr.): Celebrating; keeping festival.
en passant (Fr.): In passing.
en rapport (Fr.): In touch with; familiar with.
en suite (Fr.): In a set or series (in particular, rooms en suite).
enfant terrible (Fr.): A child (or grown-up) who always makes
　the wrong remark or does the wrong thing.
entre nous (Fr.): Between ourselves.
ex animo (L.): Sincerely; from the heart.
ex capite (L.): From memory; from the head.
ex cathedrâ (L.): From the chair; with authority.
ex gratia (L.): As an act of grace (often used as an ex gratia
　payment; i.e., a payment which did not have to be made).
exempli gratia (L.): For example (nearly always shortened to
　e.g.).

F

fait accompli (Fr.): Already done; an accomplished fact.
femme de chambre (Fr.): A chambermaid.
femme de charge (Fr.): A housekeeper.
fête champêtre (Fr.): An open-air festival; a fair.
fiacre (Fr.): A cab; a public carriage drawn by horses.
flâneur (Fr.): A lounger; wastrel.
force majeure (Fr.): Overwhelming force.
fortiter in re (L.): Firmness in action.

G

gens d'affaires (Fr.): Business men.
gitano (Sp.): Gipsy.
gourmet (Fr.): One who likes much good food.
grande parure (Fr.): Full dress.
grande monde (Fr.): High society.

H

Hausfrau (Ger.): Housewife; the lady of the house.
haute finance (Fr.): High finance.
hic jacet (L.): Here lies.
hoi polloi (Gr.): The people; the multitude.
homme de lettres (Fr.): A literary man.
honi soit qui mal y pense (Fr.): Evil to him who evil thinks (the
　motto of the Order of the Garter).

honoris causa (L.): For the honour's sake (said of honorary degrees; i.e., degrees conferred without examination on famous people).

hors de combat (Fr.): Disabled; no longer in a condition to fight.

I

ibidem (L.): In the same place (usually abbreviated to *ibid.*).

ich dien (Ger.): I serve (the motto of the Prince of Wales).

id est (L.): That is (always written **i.e.**).

idée fixe (Fr.): A fixed idea; obsession.

in actu (L.): In reality; actually.

in camera (L.): Privately; in secret.

in extremis (L.): In extreme difficulties; the last dying moments.

in loco parentis (L.): In place of a parent; guardianship.

in memoriam (L.): In memory of.

in perpetuum (L.): In perpetuity; for ever.

in re (L.): In the matter of.

in situ (L.): In its place.

in toto (L.): As a whole; entirely.

in vacuo (L): In a vacuum.

inter alia (L.): Amongst other things.

ipsissima verba (L.): The exact words (of a quotation).

ipso facto (L.): Obvious from the facts.

ipso jure (L.): In strict law.

J

jardin des plantes (Fr.): Botanical garden.

je ne sais quoi (Fr.): I know not what.

jeu de mots (Fr.): A play upon words; pun.

jour de fête (Fr.): Festival day; patron saint's day

L

læsa majestas (L.), **lèse majesté** (Fr.): High treason (generally written in English **lese-majesty**).

laissez faire (Fr.): Let alone (a term used to denote uncontrolled competition).

lapsus linguæ (L.): A slip of the tongue.

lapsus memoriæ (L.): A slip of the memory.

lares et penates (L.): Household gods.

les convenances (Fr.): The proprieties; the correct things to do

levée en masse (Fr.): A mass rising; an armed rising to repel invasion.

locum tenens (L.): A substitute; a person taking the place of someone else.

M

magnum opus (L.): A great work; the principal book of an author.

maître d'hôtel (Fr.): Hotel-keeper; house steward; sometimes used to mean a head-waiter; butler.

mal de mer (Fr.): Sea-sickness.

mañana (Sp.): Tomorrow (indicates the habit of always putting off a task until tomorrow, which never comes).

mariage de convenance (Fr.): A marriage of convenience; an arranged marriage for money or other worldly advantage.

mea culpa (L.): It is my fault.

memorabilia (L.): Things important to remember.

mens rea (L.): A guilty mind; with intent.

mise en scène (Fr.): A stage set; visible surroundings.

modus operandi (L.): A method of working; system.

multum in parvo (L.): Much in little.

N

ne plus ultra (L.): No further; nothing beyond (indicating perfection).

noblesse oblige (Fr.): Noble birth has obligations.

nom de guerre (Fr.): An assumed name.

nom de plume (Fr.): A pen-name.

non compos mentis (L.): Of unsound mind; not responsible for actions.

non sequitur (L.): It does not follow.

nota bene (L.): Note well (usually shortened to **N.B.**).

nouveau riche (Fr.): A person with newly acquired wealth; an upstart (generally spoken slightingly of someone who, despite his new wealth, has bad manners).

O

opere citato (L.): In the work named (usually abbreviated to *op. cit.*).

opus (L.): A work (usually applied to books, paintings, and musical compositions). See **magnum opus**.

outré (Fr.): In bad taste; outside what is considered acceptable.

P

pace (L.): By consent of.

par accident (Fr.): By accident.

par accord (Fr.): By agreement.

par excellence (Fr.): Very excellent; of very high standard.

par exemple (Fr.): For example.

pari mutuel (Fr.): A mutual (or pool) bet (mostly used for the system of betting by totalisator).

pari passu (L.): With equal step; side by side.

parole d'honneur (Fr.): Word of honour.

per annum (L.): By the year.

per ardua ad astra (L.): Through hardship to the stars (motto of the R.A.F.).

per capita (L.): By the head; per head.

per centum (L.): By the hundred (mostly shortened to **per cent**).

per diem (L.): By the day.

per interim (L.): Meanwhile.

per mensem (L.): By the month.

per procurationem (L.): For and on behalf of, as agent for (usually shortened to **p.p.**).

per stirpes (L.): By families.

persona grata (L.): A person in favour; an acceptable person.

persona non grata (L.): A person not in favour.

pièce de résistance (Fr.): The principal course of a dinner.

pied-à-terre (Fr.): A lodging to stay at occasionally.

post meridiem (L.): Afternoon (shortened to **p.m.**).

poste restante (Fr.): To remain until called for; a post office where packages will be held until called for.

pour prendre congé (Fr.): To take leave (shortened to **p.p.c.**, and written on a visiting card when taking leave).

prima ballerina (It.): The principal dancer in a ballet.

prima donna (It.): The principal singer in an opera.

prima facie (L.): At first sight; on first consideration.

pro forma (L.): As a matter of form.

pro rata (L.): In proportion.

procès verbal (Fr.): A written statement (used in criminal proceedings).

prosit! (Ger.): Good health!

Q

quid pro quo (L.): One thing for another of equal value.

quod erat demonstrandum (L.): Which was to be demonstrated (shortened to **Q.E.D.**).

quod erat faciendum (L.): Which was to be done (shortened to **Q.E.F.**).

quod vide (L.): Which see (shortened to **q.v.**).

R

raison d'état (Fr.): Considerations of public policy.

raison d'être (Fr.): Reason for existence.

rara avis (L.): A rare bird; a prodigy.

reductio ad absurdum (L.): Reduction to absurdity (of an argument).

rendez-vous (Fr.): A place of meeting; an appointment.

rentes (Fr.): Investments.

rentiers (Fr.): People who live upon investments.

répondez, s'il vous plaît (Fr.): Please reply (shortened to **R.S.V.P.**).

requiescat in pace (L.): Rest in peace (shortened to **R.I.P.**).

résumé (Fr.): A summary.

S

sans cérémonie (Fr.): Without ceremony.

sans doute (Fr.): Without doubt.

sauve qui peut! (Fr.): Save himself who can!

savoir-faire (Fr.): Skill in dealing with people; tact.

sic (L.): So (inserted after a quotation to indicate that it is literal).

sine die (L.): Without a day being fixed; indefinitely.

sobriquet (Fr.): Nickname.

soi-disant (Fr.): Self-styled.

sotto voce (It.): Spoken in an undertone.

status quo (L.): As things were (or are).

stet (L.): Let it stand (used when wishing a correction made in error to be ignored).

sub judice (L.): Under a judge (used in connection with a lawsuit which has not yet been decided).

sub pœna (L.): Under penalty; when written as **subpœna**, it means a summons to appear in a law court.

succès d'estime (Fr.): A success that brings honour rather than profit.

T

table d'hôte (Fr.): A set meal.
tempus fugit (L.): Time flies.
terra firma (L.): Solid earth.
tête-à-tête (Fr.): Head to head; a conversation between two people.
tour de force (Fr.): A feat of strength or skill.
tout de suite (Fr.): Immediately.
tout ensemble (Fr.): Taken altogether.

UVW

ubique (L.): Everywhere (the motto of the Royal Artillery).
ultra vires (L.): Exceeding one's legal powers.
ut infra (L.): As below.
ut supra (L.): As above.
vade mecum (L.): Constant companion (usually applied to a favourite book which is carried about everywhere).
vice versa (L.): A reversal of the order.
vide ut supra (L.): See what is stated above.
vis-à-vis (Fr.): Opposite; one's opposite number.
volente Deo (L.): God willing (shortened to **D.V.**).
wagon-lit (Fr.): A sleeping-car on a railway.

USEFUL BOOKS

THERE IS so much knowledge in the world that it is impossible for any one person to know everything. Nor is it necessary, because the world's knowledge is stored in books, from which it can always be obtained when required.

Just a few of those books are listed below. In each entry the title comes first, then the author's name (if given in the book), and finally the publisher's name in brackets.

Hobbies, Sports, and Pets

Boys' Book of Cricket, P. Pringle (Evans).
Boys' Book of Hobbies, C. Wallace (Evans).
Boys' Book of Soccer, P. Pringle (Evans).

Boys' Book of Sport, C. Wallace (Ward Lock).
Complete Home Entertainer (Odhams).
Enjoy Your Photography, C. Wallace (Evans).
Hoyle's Games Modernised, L. H. Dawson (Routledge).
Official Rules of Sports and Games (Kaye).
Photographer's Pocket Book, C. Wallace (Evans).
Right Way to Keep Dogs, R. C. G. Hancock (Andrew Elliot).
Treasury of Games and Puzzles, C. Wallace (Evans).
Wisden's Cricketers' Almanack (Sporting Handbooks).
Woodworker's Pocket Book, C. H. Hayward (Evans).
Young Collector's Handbook, E. C. R. Hadfield and C. H. Ellis (Oxford University Press).
Your Pets, V. Higgins (Westhouse).

Science and Technical

Art of Cycling, N. Spencer (Thorsons).
Boy's Book of Engines, Motors and Turbines, A. Morgan (Stanmore Press).
Boy's Book of Science and Invention (Evans).
Boy's Book of World Famous Aeroplanes (Hughes).
British Railways for Boys, C. J. Allen (Hodder).
Dictionary of Scientific Terms (Oliver and Boyd).
Driving Test Fully Explained, F. S. Hollidge (Temple Press).
Jane's All the World's Aircraft (Low).
Motor Cycles and How to Manage Them (Iliffe).
Railways, Ships and Aeroplanes (Odhams).
Teach Yourself to Fly, N. Tangye (English Universities Press).
World Railways (Sampson, Low).

Ships and Sailing

Amateur Boat Building, M. Verney (Murray).
Boy's Book of World-Famous Liners (Hughes).
Boy's Own Book of Ships, D. F. McDowell (Low).
Boy's Own Book of Warships, D. F. McDowell (Low).
Jane's Fighting Ships (Low).
Sailing and Cruising for Small Boat Owners, K. A. Coles (Batsford).

Nature

All About Birds, W. S. Berridge (Harrap).
All About Fish,   ,,   ,,

All About Reptiles, W. S. Berridge (Harrap).
Butterflies and Moths, T. Wood (Nelson).
Gardener's Pocket Book, C. Wallace (Evans).
Wild Animals in Britain, F. Pitt (Batsford).
Young Bird Watchers, A. F. C. Hillstead (Faber).

Music and Art

Drawing Dogs, D. Thorne (Studio).
Get to Know Music, J. R. Tobin (Evans).
How to Draw Ships, P. E. Anson (Studio).
How to Draw Trees, G. Brown (Studio).
How to Draw Wild Flowers, V. Temple (Studio).

General Information

Authors' and Printers' Dictionary, F. H. Collins (Oxford University Press).
Dictionary of Abbreviations, C. C. Matthews (Routledge).
Dictionary of Modern English Usage, H. W. Fowler (Oxford University Press).
Dictionary of Phrase and Fable, E. C. Brewer (Cassell).
Encyclopædia Britannica.
Everyman's Encyclopædia (Dent).
Facts and How to Find Them, W. A. Bagley (Pitmans).
Oxford Dictionary of Quotations (Oxford University Press).
Oxford Junior Encyclopædia (Oxford University Press).
Pictorial Treasury, C. Wallace (Evans)
Pictorial Treasury II: The British Commonwealth, C. Wallace (Evans)
Scholarship Guide (Associated Newspapers).
Thesaurus of English Words and Phrases, P. M. Roget (Longmans).
Twentieth Century Dictionary (Chambers).
Whitaker's Almanack (Whitaker).
Willing's Press Guide (Willings).

TABLES AND FORMULÆ

WEIGHTS AND MEASURES

English System

Length

12 inches	.	.	.	.	= 1 foot
3 feet .	.	.	.	.	= 1 yard
$5\frac{1}{2}$ yards	.	.	.	.	= 1 pole
22 yards	.	.	.	.	= 1 chain
220 yards	.	.	.	.	= 1 furlong
8 furlongs	.	.	.	.	= 1 mile

(The mile = 1,760 yards = 5,280 feet)

Area

144 sq. inches .	.	= 1 sq. foot
9 sq. feet .	.	= 1 sq. yard
$30\frac{1}{4}$ sq. yards	.	= 1 rod, pole or perch
40 perches .	.	= 1 rood
4 roods .	.	= 1 acre
640 acres .	.	= 1 sq. mile

(1 rood = 1,210 sq. yds. and
1 acre = 4,840 sq. yds.)

Volume

1,728 cubic inches	.	= 1 cubic foot
27 cubic feet .	.	= I cubic yard

Length at Sea

6 feet .	.	= 1 fathom
100 fathoms	.	= 1 cable
10 cables	.	= 1 nautical mile

(1 nautical mile = 6,080 ft. 1 knot = 1 n.
mile per hour; i.e., it is a speed, not a distance)

Angles

60 seconds (″)	.	.	. = 1 minute (′)
60 minutes	.	.	. = 1 degree (°)
90 degrees	.	.	. = 1 right angle
4 right angles	.	.	. = 1 circle (360°)

Avoirdupois

16 drams (dr.)	.	= 1 ounce (oz.)
16 ounces	.	= 1 pound (lb.)
14 pounds	.	= 1 stone
28 pounds	.	= 1 quarter (qr.)
4 quarters	.	= 1 hundredweight (cwt.)
20 hundredweights		= 1 ton

7,000 grains	.	= 1 pound
112 pounds	.	= 1 hundredweight
2,240 pounds	.	= 1 ton

Apothecaries' (*Used for drugs*)

20 grains	.	.	= 1 scruple (Ə)
3 scruples	.	.	= 1 drachm (Ʒ)
8 drachms	.	.	= 1 ounce

60 minims	.	.	= 1 fluid drachm
8 fluid drachms	.	.	= 1 fluid ounce
20 fluid ounces	.	.	= 1 pint

(The Apothecaries' grain is the same as the Avoirdupois grain, but the Ap. oz. is the Troy oz.)

Troy (*Used for precious metals*)

24 grains	.	.	= 1 pennyweight (dwt.)
20 pennyweights	.		= 1 ounce

Capacity

All Liquids

4 gills	.	.	.	= 1 pint
2 pints	.	.	.	= 1 quart
4 quarts	.	.	.	= 1 gallon

For Wine only

10 gallons	.	.	.	= 1 anker
42 gallons	.	.	.	= 1 tierce
1½ tierces	.	.	.	= 1 hogshead
2 tierces	.	.	.	= 1 puncheon
2 hogsheads	.	.	.	= 1 pipe
2 pipes	.	.	.	= 1 tun

For Solids only

2 gallons	.	.	= 1 peck
8 gallons	.	.	= 1 bushel
8 bushels	.	.	= 1 quarter

Metric

Length

10 millimetres (mm.)	=	1 centimetre (cm.)
10 centimetres	.	= 1 decimetre (dm.)
10 decimetres	.	= 1 metre (m.)
10 metres	.	= 1 dekametre (dam.)
10 dekametres	.	= 1 hectometre (hm.)
10 hectometres	.	= 1 kilometre (km.)

Area (Land)

100 sq. metres	.	= 1 are (a.)
100 ares	.	= 1 hectare (ha.)
100 hectares	.	= 1 sq. kilometre

Weight

10 milligrams (mg.)	=	1 centigram (cg.)
10 centigrams	.	= 1 decigram (dg.)
10 decigrams	.	= 1 gramme (grm.)
10 grammes	.	= 1 dekagram (dag.)
10 dekagrams	.	= 1 hectogram (hg.)
10 hectograms	.	= 1 kilogram (kg.)
10 kilograms	.	= 1 myriagram
10 myriagrams	.	= 1 quintal (q.)
10 quintals	.	= 1 tonne (t.)

(Jewellers weigh their gems in carats. 1 carat
= 200 milligrams.)

Capacity

10 millilitres (mil.)	.	=	1 centilitre (cl.)
10 centilitres	.	=	1 decilitre (dl.)
10 decilitres	.	=	1 litre (lit.)
10 litres	.	=	1 dekalitre (dal.)
10 dekalitres	.	=	1 hectolitre (hl.)

CONVERSION TABLES

English

Length

1 inch	.	=	25·400 millimetres
1 foot	.	=	0·30480 metre
1 yard	.	=	0·914383 metre
1 fathom	.	=	1·8288 metres
1 pole	.	=	5·0292 „
1 chain	.	=	20·1168 „
1 furlong	.	=	201·168 „
1 mile	.	=	1·6093 kilometres

Area

1 sq. in.	.	=	6·4516 sq. centimetres
1 sq. ft.	.	=	9·2903 sq. decimetres
1 sq. yd.	.	=	0·8361 sq. metre
1 perch	.	=	25·293 sq. metres
1 rood	.	=	10·117 ares
1 ac.	.	=	0·40468 hectare
1 sq. mile	.	=	259·00 hectares

Volume

1 cub. in.	.	=	16·387 cub. centimetres
1 cub. ft.	.	=	0·028317 cub. metre
1 cub. yd.	.	=	0·764553 „ „

Capacity

1 gill	.	=	1·42 decilitres
1 pint	.	=	0·568 litre
1 quart	.	=	1·136 litres

1 gallon . . .	= 4·54596 litres
1 peck . . .	= 9·092 litres
1 bushel . . .	= 3·637 decalitres
1 quarter . . .	= 2·900 hectolitres

Avoirdupois

1 grain . . .	= 0·0648 gramme
1 dram . . .	= 1·772 grammes
1 ounce . . .	= 28·350 ,,
1 pound . . .	= 0·453 kilogram
1 stone . . .	= 6·350 kilograms
1 quarter . . .	= 12·70 ,,
1 hundredweight .	= 50·80 ,,
1 ton . . .	= 1,017 ,,

Apothecaries'

1 minim . . .	= 0·059 millilitre
1 fluid scruple . .	= 1·184 millilitres
1 fluid drachm . .	= 3·552 ,,
1 fluid ounce . .	= 2·84123 centilitres
1 pint . . .	= 0·568 litre

1 grain . . .	= 0·648 gramme
1 scruple (20 grains) .	= 1·296 grammes
1 drachm (3 scruples)	= 3·888 ,,
1 oz. (8 drachms) .	= 31·1035 ,,

Troy

1 grain . . .	= 0·0648 gramme
1 pennyweight . .	= 1·5552 grammes
1 troy ounce . .	= 31·1035 ,,
1 troy pound . .	= 373·2420 ,,

Metric

Length

1 millimetre . .	= 0·03937 inch
1 centimetre . .	= 0·3937 ,,
1 decimetre . .	= 3·937 inches
1 metre . . .	= $\begin{cases} 3\cdot28084 \text{ feet} \\ 1\cdot0936 \text{ yards} \end{cases}$

1 decametre	.	.	=	10·936 yards
1 hectometre	.	.	=	109·36 ,,
1 kilometre	.	.	=	0·62137 mile

Area

1 square centimetre	.	=	0·15500 sq. in.
1 sq. decimetre	.	=	15·500 sq. in.
1 sq. metre	.	=	$\begin{cases} 10\cdot7639 \text{ sq. ft.} \\ 1\cdot1960 \text{ sq. yds.} \end{cases}$
1 are	. .	=	119·60 ,, ,,
1 hectare	. .	=	2·4711 acres

Volume

1 cubic centimetre	.	=	0·061 cubic in.
1 cubic decimetre (c.d.) (1,000 cub. centimetres) .	$\Big\}$	=	61·024 cubic in.
1 cub. metre (1,000 cub. decimetres)	$\Big\}$	=	$\begin{cases} 35\cdot3166 \text{ cubic ft.} \\ 1\cdot307954 \text{ ,, yds.} \end{cases}$

Capacity

1 centilitre	.	.	=	0·07 gill
1 decilitre	.	.	=	0·176 pint
1 litre	.	.	=	1·7598 pints
1 decalitre	.	.	=	2·2 gallons
1 hectolitre	.	.	=	2·75 bushels

Weight

Avoirdupois

1 milligramme	.	.	=	0·015 grain
1 centigramme	.	.	=	0·154 ,,
1 decigramme	.	.	=	1·543 grains
1 gramme	.	.	=	15·432 ,,
1 decagramme	.	.	=	5·644 drams.
1 hectogramme	.	.	=	3·527 oz.
1 kilogram	.	.	=	2·2046 lb.
1 myriagram	.	.	=	22·046 lb.
1 quintal	.	.	=	1·968 cwt.
1 tonne	.	.	=	0·984 ton

Weight

$$1 \text{ gramme} \quad . \quad . \quad = \begin{cases} \textit{Troy} \\ 0 \cdot 03215 \text{ oz. troy} \\ 15 \cdot 432 \text{ grains} \end{cases}$$

$$1 \text{ gramme} \quad . \quad . \quad = \begin{cases} \textit{Apothecaries'} \\ 0 \cdot 2572 \text{ drachm} \\ 0 \cdot 7716 \text{ scruple} \\ 15 \cdot 432 \text{ grains} \end{cases}$$

ROUGH CONVERSIONS

(Very approximate; intended for rough calculations only)

1 inch	. . . =	2½ centimetres
1 foot	. . . =	30 ,,
1 acre	. . . =	4 decares
1 grain	. . . =	6½ centigrams
1 lb.	. . . =	0·45 kilogram
7 quarts	. . . =	8 litres
1 metre	. . . =	39½ inches
1 kilometre	. . . =	⅝ mile
1 kilogram	. . . =	2·2 lb.
1 litre	. . . =	1¾ pints

MISCELLANEOUS MEASURES

1 *gallon* of pure water weighs 10 lb.

A hand (when measuring a horse) is 4 ins.

A reputed quart (as in a bottle of wine, or spirit) is one-sixth of a gallon.

The gramme (Metric) is the weight of 1 cub. cm. of pure water.

The litre (Metric) is 1,000 cub. cm. of pure water, and weighs 1 kilogram.

The British Thermal Unit (B.Th.U.) is the amount of heat required to raise 1lb. of water by 1° F.

The Therm = 100,000 B.Th.U.

The horsepower (h.p.) is the power needed to raise 550 lbs. one foot in one second (or 33,000 lbs. one foot in one minute).

The kilowatt (1,000 watts) is the power needed to raise 737·6 lb. one foot in one second (746 watts = 1 h.p.).

The Unit (Board of Trade unit, or B.O.T.U.) is consumption of electricity equal to 1,000 watts for one hour.

Foreign

U.S.A.—Two tons are in use, a long ton of 2,240 lb. (the English ton) and a short ton of 2,000 lb., which is divided into 20 units of 100 lb.

U.S.S.R.—Distance is measured by the verst (= 1,166 yds. or about $\frac{2}{3}$ mile). Weight is by the funt (0·9 lb.); 40 funts = about 36 lb.

South Africa.—Some of the old Boer measures are still used, in particular the morgen (2·1165 acres) and the leaguer (about 128 gallons). The South African anker (Boer) is only $7\frac{1}{2}$ gallons.

British Coins as Weights and Measures

3 pennies	= 1 oz.
5 halfpennies	= 1 oz.
10 farthings	= 1 oz.
1 halfpenny	= 1 inch

MEASURES OF NUMBER

Articles

12	= 1 dozen
20	= 1 score
5 score	= 1 hundred
6 score	= 1 great hundred
12 dozen	= 1 gross
12 gross	= 1 great gross

Paper

24 sheets	= 1 quire
20 quires	= 1 ream

(*Note:* Stationers' reams are generally 480 sheets; printers' reams are 500 or 516 sheets.)

THERMOMETER MARKINGS

THERE ARE three markings for thermometers: Fahrenheit, Centigrade, and Réaumur.

The Fahrenheit marking is the one in general use throughout the British Empire and the United States; it shows 212° for boiling water and 32° for ice.

The Centigrade marking is the one used in Europe, and it is also used in scientific work; it shows 100° for boiling water and 0° for ice.

The Réaumur marking was at one time used in France, but its place was taken by the Centigrade marking, and it is no longer popular. It shows 80° for boiling water and 0° for ice.

Conversion Rules

To convert a Fahrenheit reading to Centigrade, subtract 32, multiply by 5, and divide by 9.

To convert a Centigrade reading to Fahrenheit, multiply by 9, divide by 5, and add 32.

The particular marking for any thermometer is shown by the letter F for Fahrenheit and the letter C for Centigrade. Thus boiling water is 212° F. or 100° C. For temperatures lower than zero on both scales, the minus sign is used; thus −5° F. or −20° C. Comparison between the Fahrenheit and Centigrade markings is shown in the drawings above.

The lowest temperature believed possible (called the *absolute zero of temperature*) is −273° C. The highest temperature, apart from that of an atomic explosion, is found in the flame of an electric arc: 5,000° C. The average temperature of the blood of a healthy human being is 98·4° F. (36·9° C.).

SQUARES, CUBES, SQUARE ROOTS, CUBE ROOTS, AND RECIPROCALS

N	N^2	N^3	$\sqrt{N}$	$\sqrt[3]{N}$	$\dfrac{1}{N}$
1	1	1	1·0	1·0	1·0
2	4	8	1·414	1·26	0·5
3	9	27	1·732	1·442	0·3333
4	16	64	2·0	1·587	0·25
5	25	125	2·236	1·71	0·2
6	36	216	2·49	1·817	0·1667
7	49	343	2·646	1·913	0·1429
8	64	512	2·828	2·0	0·125
9	81	729	3·0	2·08	0·1111
10	100	1,000	3·162	2·154	0·1
11	121	1,331	3·317	2·224	0·0909
12	144	1,728	3·464	2·289	0·0833
13	169	2,197	3·606	2·351	0·0769
14	196	2,744	3·742	2·41	0·0714
15	225	3,375	3·873	2·466	0·0667
16	256	4,096	4·0	2·52	0·0625
17	289	4,913	4·123	2·571	0·0588
18	324	5,832	4·243	2·621	0·0556
19	361	6,859	4·359	2·668	0·0526
20	400	8,000	4·472	2·714	0·05
21	441	9,261	4·583	2·759	0·0476
22	484	10,648	4·69	2·802	0·0455
23	529	12,167	4·796	2·844	0·0435
24	576	13,824	4·899	2·885	0·0417
25	625	15,625	5·0	2·924	0·04
26	676	17,576	5·099	2·962	0·0385
27	729	19,683	5·196	3·0	0·037
28	784	21,952	5·292	3·037	0·0357
29	841	24,389	5·385	3·072	0·0345
30	900	27,000	5·477	3·107	0·0333
31	961	29,791	5·568	3·141	0·0323
32	1,024	32,768	5·657	3·175	0·0313
33	1,089	35,937	5·745	3·208	0·0303
34	1,156	39,304	5·831	3·24	0·0294
35	1,225	42,875	5·916	3·271	0·0286
36	1,296	46,656	6·0	3·302	0·0278

37	1,369	50,653	6·083	3·332	0·027
38	1,444	54,872	6·164	3·362	0·0263
39	1,521	59,319	6·245	3·391	0·0256
40	1,600	64,000	6·325	3·42	0·025
41	1,681	68,921	6·403	3·448	0·024
42	1,764	74,088	6·481	3·476	0·0238
43	1,849	79,507	6·557	3·503	0·0233
44	1,936	85,184	6·633	3·53	0·0227
45	2,025	91,125	6·708	3·557	0·0222
46	2,116	97,336	6·782	3·583	0·0217
47	2,209	103,823	6·856	3·609	0·0213
48	2,304	110,592	6·928	3·634	0·0208
49	2,401	117,649	7·0	3·659	0·0204
50	2,500	125,000	7·071	3·684	0·02

ROMAN NUMERALS

ROMAN NUMERALS are often used to denote dates on buildings and books, and the hours on clock-faces.

The symbols for Roman numerals are: I = 1; V = 5;
X = 10; L = 50; C = 100; D = 500; and M = 1,000.

The symbols are simply added together to arrive at the
total value; but when a symbol of lesser value appears immediately in front of one of higher value, that symbol is
subtracted. For example: IV = V minus I = 4.

Below are a number of values in Roman numerals shown
against their corresponding values in ordinary figures.

I	—	1	XV	—	15	CL	—	150
II	—	2	XVI	—	16	CC	—	200
III	—	3	XVII	—	17	CD	—	400
IV	—	4	XVIII	—	18	D	—	500
V	—	5	XIX	—	19	DC	—	600
VI	—	6	XX	—	20	CM	—	900
VII	—	7	XXX	—	30	M	—	1,000
VIII	—	8	XL	—	40	MC	—	1,100
IX	—	9	L	—	50	MCC	—	1,200
X	—	10	LX	—	60	MD	—	1,500
XI	—	11	LXX	—	70	ML	—	1,050
XII	—	12	LXXX	—	80	MM	—	2,000
XIII	—	13	XC	—	90	MCMLX	—	1,960
XIV	—	14	C	—	100			

THE GREEK ALPHABET

THIS ALPHABET is important because its letters are used so
often in mathematics (π is a good example), and in science
generally.   The word "alphabet" itself is derived from the
first two Greek letters.

There are no Greek equivalents of our c, h, j, q, v, and w.

Name	Letter		English Equivalent
Alpha	**A**	α	a
Beta	**B**	β	b
Gamma	**Γ**	γ	g (*hard*)
Delta	**Δ**	δ	d
Epsilon	**E**	ϵ	e (*short*)
Zeta	**Z**	ζ	z, dz
Eta	**H**	η	e (*long*)
Theta	**Θ**	θ, ϑ	th
Iota	**I**	ι	i
Kappa	**K**	$\varkappa$	k, *or hard* c
Lambda	**Λ**	λ	l
Mu	**M**	μ	m
Nu	**N**	ν	n
Xi	**Ξ**	ξ	x
Omicron	**O**	o	o (*short*)
Pi	**Π**	π	p
Rho	**P**	ρ	r
Sigma	**Σ**	σ, ς	s
Tau	**T**	τ	t
Upsilon	**Y**	υ	u *or* y
Phi	**Φ**	φ	ph, f
Chi	**X**	χ	kh *or hard* ch
Psi	**Ψ**	ψ	ps
Omega	**Ω**	ω	o (*long*)

MATHEMATICAL SIGNS

Is equal to	.	.	.	$=$	Not greater than . .	$\not>$
Is not equal to	.	.	.	$\neq$	Less than . . .	$<$
Is approx. equal to	.	.	.	$\fallingdotseq$	Not less than . .	$\not<$
Is the same as	.	.	.	$\equiv$	The sum of . .	Σ
The difference between	.	.	.	$\sim$	Sign of an angle . .	θ

Varies as				$\propto$	A small difference		δ
Greater than			$>$		Angle		$\wedge$

USEFUL FORMULÆ

(where b = base; h = perpendicular height; r = radius; d = diameter)

Simple Areas and Volumes

Square = b^2 (or h^2)
Triangle = $\frac{1}{2}bh$
Parallelogram = bh
Rhomboid = bh

Circles and Spheres

(*see below for value of* π)

Circle—circumference = $2\pi r$ (or πd).
   area = πr^2
Sphere—area of surface = $4\pi r^2$
   volume = $4/3\pi r^3$

Cylinders and Cones

Cylinder—volume = $\pi r^2 h$
Cone—volume = $1/3\pi r^2 h$

Functions of π

$$\pi = 3{\cdot}14159 \left(or\ 3{\cdot}1416\ or\ \frac{22}{7}\right)$$

$2\pi = 6{\cdot}2832$	$3\pi = 9{\cdot}4248$
$\pi^2 = 9{\cdot}8696$	$\pi^3 = 31{\cdot}006$
$\dfrac{\pi}{2} = 1{\cdot}5708$	$\dfrac{\pi}{4} = 0{\cdot}7854$
$\dfrac{\pi}{6} = 0{\cdot}5236$	$\dfrac{4}{3}\pi = 4{\cdot}1888$
$\dfrac{1}{\pi} = 0{\cdot}3183$	$\dfrac{1}{2\pi} = 0{\cdot}1592$
$\sqrt{\pi} = 1{\cdot}7725$	$\sqrt[3]{\pi} = 1{\cdot}4646$

$$\frac{1}{\sqrt{\pi}} = 0.5642 \qquad\qquad \frac{1}{\pi^2} = 0.1013$$

$$\log \pi = 0.4971$$

Trigonometrical Ratios

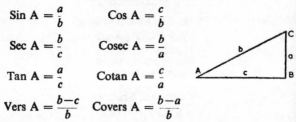

$$\text{Sin A} = \frac{a}{b} \qquad\qquad \text{Cos A} = \frac{c}{b}$$

$$\text{Sec A} = \frac{b}{c} \qquad\qquad \text{Cosec A} = \frac{b}{a}$$

$$\text{Tan A} = \frac{a}{c} \qquad\qquad \text{Cotan A} = \frac{c}{a}$$

$$\text{Vers A} = \frac{b-c}{b} \qquad\qquad \text{Covers A} = \frac{b-a}{b}$$

Mechanics

Falling Bodies

$$v = u + gt$$

$$h = \frac{u+v}{2}t$$

$$h = ut + \tfrac{1}{2}gt^2$$

$$g = \frac{v-u}{t}$$

where g = gravity = 32 (in ft. per sec. per sec.)
u = initial velocity (in ft. per sec.),
v = final velocity (in ft. per sec.),
h = height (in feet).
t = time (in secs.)

Pendulum

$$t = 2\pi \sqrt{\frac{l}{g}}$$

where t = time of complete swing (once in each direction)
in secs.,
l = length of pendulum (in ft.),
g = gravity (as above).

Electricity

Ohm's Law

$$V = IR \qquad R = \frac{V}{I} \qquad I = \frac{V}{R}$$

$$W = IV = I^2R = \frac{V^2}{R}$$

where V = volts, I = current (in amperes), R = resistance in ohms, and W = watts.

Resistances

in series, $R = R_1 + R_2 + R_3$, etc.

in parallel, $\dfrac{1}{R} = \dfrac{1}{R_1} + \dfrac{1}{R_2} + \dfrac{1}{R_3}$, etc.

Condensers

in series, $\dfrac{1}{C} = \dfrac{1}{C_1} + \dfrac{1}{C_2} + \dfrac{1}{C_3}$, etc.

in parallel, $C = C_1 + C_2 + C_3$, etc.

where C = capacity (in farads or in microfarads).

Frequency and Wavelength

$$f = \frac{300,000}{\lambda}, \text{ and } \lambda = \frac{300,000}{f}$$

where f = frequency (in kilocycles) and λ = wavelength (in metres).

CHEMICAL FORMULÆ
(Usual Laboratory Compounds)

Acetaldehyde	CH_3CHO
Acetone	$CH_3CO \cdot CH_3$
Acetylene	C_2H_2
Acid—Acetic	CH_3COOH
„ Boric	H_3BO_3
„ Citric	$C_3H_4(OH)(COOH)_3$
„ Formic	$H \cdot COOH$
„ Gallic	$C_6H_2(OH)_3COOH$
„ Hydrochloric	HCl

S.P.B.—8

Acid—Nitric	HNO_3
„ Nitrous	HNO_2
„ Oxalic	$(COOH)_2,2H_2O$
„ Phosphoric	H_3PO_4
„ Phosphorous	H_3PO_3
„ Sulphuric	H_2SO_4
„ Sulphurous	H_2SO_3
Alcohol—Ethyl	CH_3CH_2OH
„ Methyl	CH_3OH
Aluminium Ammonium Sulphate	$NH_4Al(SO_4)_2$
„ Chloride	$AlCl_3$
„ Hydroxide	$Al(OH)_3$
„ Oxide	Al_2O_3
„ Potassium Sulphate	$KAl(SO_4)_2$
„ Sulphate	$Al_2(SO_4)_3$
Ammonia	NH_3
Ammonium Carbonate	$(NH_4)_2CO_3$
„ Chloride	NH_4Cl
„ Nitrate	NH_4NO_3
„ Sulphate	$(NH_4)_2SO_4$
Amyl Acetate	$CH_3COOC_5H_{11}$
Aniline	$C_6H_5NH_2$
Barium Chloride	$BaCl_2$
„ Hydroxide	$Ba(OH)_2$
„ Sulphate	$BaSO_4$
Benzaldehyde	C_6H_5CHO
Benzene	C_6H_6
Borax	$Na_2B_4O_7$
Bromoform	$CHBr_3$
Calcium Bromide	$CaBr_2$
„ Carbide	CaC_2
„ Carbonate	$CaCO_3$
„ Chloride	$CaCl_2$
„ Hydroxide	$Ca(OH)_2$
„ Oxide	CaO
„ Sulphate	$CaSO_4$
„ Sulphide	CaS
Carbon Dioxide	CO_2
Carbon Tetrachloride	CCl_4
Chloroform	$CHCl_3$
Chrome Alum	$KCr(SO_4)_2$

Chromium Oxide	Cr_2O_3
Copper Nitrate	$Cu(NO_3)_2$
,, Oxide (Cupric)	CuO
,, Oxide (Cuprous)	Cu_2O
,, Sulphate	$CuSO_4$
,, Sulphide	CuS
Dextrose	$C_6H_{12}O_6$
Ether	$(C_2H_5)_2O$
Ethyl Chloride	C_2H_5Cl
Ferric Ammonium Sulphate	$NH_4Fe(SO_4)_2$
,, Chloride	$FeCl_3$
,, Hydroxide	$Fe(OH)_3$
,, Oxide	Fe_2O_3
Ferrous Carbonate	$FeCO_3$
,, Oxide	FeO
,, Sulphate	$FeSO_4$
Formaldehyde	$H \cdot CHO$
Glycerin	$CH_2OH \cdot CHOH \cdot CH_2OH$
Hydrogen Peroxide	H_2O_2
,, Sulphide	H_2S
Iodoform	CHI_3
Lactose	$C_{12}H_{22}O_{11}$
Lead Acetate	$(CH_3COO)_2Pb$
,, Carbonate (basic)	$2PbCO_3 \cdot Pb(OH)_2$
,, Monoxide (Litharge)	PbO
,, Oxide (Red Lead)	Pb_3O_4
,, Sulphate	$PbSO_4$
,, Sulphide	PbS
Magnesium Chloride	$MgCl_2$
,, Hydroxide	$Mg(OH)_2$
,, Oxide	MgO
,, Peroxide	MgO_2
,, Phosphate	$Mg_3(PO_4)_2$
,, Sulphate	$MgSO_4$
Manganese Dioxide	MnO_2
Mercuric Oxide	HgO
,, Sulphate	$HgSO_4$
Mercurous Sulphate	Hg_2SO_4
Methane	CH_4
Methyl Chloride	CH_3Cl
,, Iodide	CH_3I

Naphthalene	$C_{11}H_8$
Nickel Oxide	NiO
Nitric Oxide	NO
Nitrobenzene	$C_6H_5NO_2$
Nitrous Oxide	N_2O
Phenol	C_6H_5OH
Phenolphthalein	$C_{22}H_{14}O_4$
Potassium Bicarbonate	$KHCO_3$
,, Bichromate	$K_2Cr_2O_7$
,, Bromide	KBr
,, Carbonate	K_2CO_3
,, Chlorate	$KClO_3$
,, Chloride	KCl
,, Chromate	K_2CrO_4
,, Hypophosphite	KPH_2O_2
,, Iodide	KI
,, Manganate	K_2MnO_4
,, Nitrate	KNO_3
,, Nitrite	KNO_2
,, Permanganate	$KMnO_4$
,, Sulphate	K_2SO_4
,, Sulphide	K_2S_3
Quinol	$C_6H_4(OH)_2$
Saccharin	$C_6H_4CO \cdot SO_2NH$
Sodium Bicarbonate	$NaHCO_3$
,, Bromide	$NaBr$
,, Carbonate	Na_2CO_3
,, Chlorate	$NaClO_3$
,, Chloride	$NaCl$
,, Hydroxide	$NaOH$
,, Hypophosphite	$NaPH_2O_2$
,, Nitrate	$NaNO_3$
,, Nitrite	$NaNO_2$
,, Phosphate	Na_2HPO_4
,, Sulphate	Na_2SO_4
,, Sulphite	Na_2SO_3
,, Thiosulphate	$Na_2S_2O_3$
Stannic Oxide	SnO_2
Strontium Carbonate	$SrCO_3$
,, Chloride	$SrCl_2$
,, Nitrate	$Sr(NO_3)_2$

Sucrose	$C_{12}H_{22}O_{11}$
Sulphur Dioxide	SO_2
,, Trioxide	SO_3
Trinitrophenol	$C_6H_2(OH)(NO_2)_3$
Water	H_2O
Zinc Chloride	$ZnCl_2$
,, Oxide	ZnO
,, Sulphate	$ZnSO_4$

Chemical Indicators

These Indicators are for use when it is wished to find out whether a substance is acid, alkaline, or neutral. When an Indicator is added to any substance, the colour it turns will show the quality of the substance as in the following table:

Indicator	Acid	Alkaline	Neutral
Litmus	Red	Blue	Purple
Methyl Orange	Pink	Yellow	Orange
Phenolphthalein	Colourless	Red	Colourless

TABLE OF ELEMENTS

IN the list below is shown all the elements which have so far been discovered—ninety-six in all. The two marked * are known to exist, but up to now nobody has succeeded in isolating them, hence their atomic weights have not been determined.

Element	Symbol	Atomic No.	Atomic Wt.	Element	Symbol	Atomic No.	Atomic Wt.
Hydrogen	H	1	1·008	Magnesium	Mg	12	24·32
Helium	He	2	4·00	Aluminium	Al	13	26·97
Lithium	Li	3	6·94	Silicon	Si	14	28·06
Beryllium	Be	4	9·02	Phosphorus	P	15	30·98
Boron	B	5	10·82	Sulphur	S	16	32·06
Carbon	C	6	12·01	Chlorine	Cl	17	35·46
Nitrogen	N	7	14·0	Argon	A	18	39·94
Oxygen	O	8	16·00	Potassium	K	19	39·09
Fluorine	F	9	19·00	Calcium	Ca	20	40·08
Neon	Ne	10	20·18	Scandium	Sc	21	45·10
Sodium	Na	11	22·97	Titanium	Ti	22	47·90

Element	Symbol	Atomic No.	Atomic Wt.	Element	Symbol	Atomic No.	Atomic Wt.
Vanadium	V	23	50·95	Neodymium	Nd	60	144·27
Chromium	Cr	24	52·01	Illinium	Il	61	146·00
Manganese	Mn	25	54·93	Samarium	Sa	62	150·43
Iron	Fe	26	55·85	Europium	Eu	63	152·00
Cobalt	Co	27	58·94	Gadolinium	Gd	64	156·90
Nickel	Ni	28	58·69	Terbium	Tb	65	159·20
Copper	Cu	29	63·57	Dysprosium	Dy	66	162·46
Zinc	Zn	30	65·38	Holmium	Ho	67	164·94
Gallium	Ga	31	69·72	Erbium	Er	68	167·20
Germanium	Ge	32	72·60	Thulium	Tm	69	169·40
Arsenic	As	33	74·91	Ytterbium	Yb	70	173·04
Selenium	Se	34	78·96	Lutecium	Lu	71	174·99
Bromine	Br	35	79·92	Hafnium	Hf	72	178·60
Krypton	Kr	36	83·70	Tantalum	Ta	73	180·88
Rubidium	Rb	37	85·48	Tungsten	W	74	183·92
Strontium	Sr	38	87·63	Rhenium	Re	75	186·31
Yttrium	Y	39	88·92	Osmium	Os	76	190·20
Zirconium	Zr	40	91·22	Iridium	Ir	77	193·10
Niobium	Nb	41	92·91	Platinum	Pt	78	195·23
Molybdenum	Mo	42	95·95	Gold	Au	79	197·20
Masurium	Ma	43	98·00	Mercury	Hg	80	200·61
Ruthenium	Ru	44	101·70	Thallium	Tl	81	204·39
Rhodium	Rh	45	102·91	Lead	Pb	82	207·21
Palladium	Pd	46	106·70	Bismuth	Bi	83	209·00
Silver	Ag	47	107·88	Polonium	Po	84	210·00
Cadmium	Cd	48	112·41	*Alabamine	Ab	85	—
Indium	In	49	114·76	Radon (Niton)	Nt	86	222·00
Tin	Sn	50	118·70	*Virginium	Vi	87	—
Antimony	Sb	51	121·76	Radium	Ra	88	226·05
Tellurium	Te	52	127·61	Actinium	Ac	89	227·00
Iodine	I	53	126·91	Thorium	Th	90	232·12
Xenon	Xe	54	131·30	Protoactinium	Pa	91	231·00
Caesium	Cs	55	132·91	Uranium	U	92	238·07
Barium	Ba	56	137·36	Neptunium	Np	93	237·00
Lanthanum	La	57	138·92	Plutonium	Pl	94	238·00
Cerium	Ce	58	140·13	Americium	Am	95	241·00
Praseodymium	Pr	59	140·92	Curium	Cm	96	242·00

New elements are: Berkelium (97), Californium (98), Unnamed (99), Unnamed (100), and Mendelevium (101).

Chemical Names of Familiar Substances

Many substances we use or talk about in everyday life are quite simple chemicals; but some, as bought in a shop in the ordinary way, are often in a slightly impure state.

If those substances were required in an absolutely pure form they would have to be obtained from a chemist, in which case their chemical names would have to be used when ordering. These chemical names and the corresponding formulæ are shown below.

Accumulator acid	Dilute sulphuric acid ($H_2SO_4 + H_2O$). Pure acid and distilled water are used, and the solution should have a specific gravity of about 1·250.
Alcohol	Ethyl alcohol (C_2H_5OH).
Alum	Aluminium potassium sulphate ($KAl(SO_4)_2$).
Aqua fortis	Nitric acid (HNO_3).
Baking powder	Bicarbonate of soda ($NaHCO_3$).
Blue vitriol	Copper sulphate, crystallised ($CuSO_4,5H_2O$).
Boracic acid	Boric acid (H_3BO_3).
Borax	Sodium borate ($Na_2B_4O_7$).
Bromide	Potassium bromide (KBr).
Carbolic acid	Phenol (C_6H_5OH).
Carbonic acid gas	Carbon dioxide (CO_2).
Caustic soda	Sodium hydroxide ($NaOH$).
Chalk	Calcium carbonate ($CaCO_3$).
Common salt	Sodium chloride ($NaCl$).
Corrosive sublimate	Mercuric chloride ($HgCl_2$).
Epsom salts	Magnesium sulphate ($MgSO_4,7H_2O$).
Firedamp	Methane (CH_4).
Glauber salts	Sodium sulphate (Na_2SO_4).
Graphite	A form of Carbon.
Green vitriol	Ferrous sulphate ($FeSO_4,7H_2O$).
Hypo	Sodium thiosulphate ($Na_2S_2O_3,5H_2O$).
Lime	Calcium oxide (CaO).
Magnesia	Magnesium oxide (MgO).
Nitre	Potassium nitrate (KNO_3).
Oil of vitriol	Sulphuric acid (H_2SO_4).

Plaster of Paris	Calcium sulphate ($CaSO_4$).
Quicklime	Calcium oxide (CaO).
Red lead	Red lead oxide (Pb_3O_4).
Salammoniac	Ammonium chloride (NH_4Cl).
Saltpetre	Potassium nitrate (KNO_3).
Sal volatile	Ammonium carbonate ($[NH_4]_2CO_3$).
Salts of lemon	Potassium hydrogen oxalate (KHC_2O_4).
Spirits of salts	Hydrochloric acid (HCl).
Sugar of lead	Lead acetate ($Pb[C_2H_3O_2]_2$).
Vinegar	Acetic acid, diluted ($C_2H_4O_2 + H_2O$).
Washing soda	Sodium carbonate, crystallised ($Na_2CO_3,10H_2O$).
White lead	Lead carbonate, basic ($2PbCO_3,Pb(OH)_2$).

Part II

HOBBIES · PASTIMES
SPORT

Index to Part II

THE COMPASS

THE MAGNETIC COMPASS, the instrument which navigators use to get from one place to another, is marked in three different ways for different purposes, and the compass card

A COMPASS CARD marked in quadrantal notation with point notation shown round the edge.

shown here gives two of them.   The three systems of marking are:

Circular Notation, in which, starting from North and moving clockwise, the compass circle is marked from 0° to 359° —often used to denote True (i.e., map) bearings, and by pilots of aircraft for setting courses.

Quadrantal Notation, in which the compass circle is marked 0° at North and South and 90° at East and West, courses being stated in degrees thus: N.45°E. (= N.E.), or S.67½°W. (= S.W. by W.). This notation is the most commonly used for steering by helmsmen on big ships at sea.

Point Notation, in which the compass circle is divided into 32 named points. Starting from North and moving clockwise, these points are shown below, together with their equivalents in Circular and Quadrantal Notations. Point Notation is used in small vessels (yachts, etc.) where steering cannot be so fine as in degrees.

Point Notation	Equivalent in Circular	Equivalent in Quadrantal	Point Notation	Equivalent in Circular	Equivalent in Quadrantal
N.	0	N.	S.	180	S.
N. by E.	11¼	N.11¼E.	S. by W.	191¼	S.11¼W.
N.N.E.	22½	N.22½E.	S.S.W.	202½	S.22½W.
N.E. by N.	33¾	N.33¾E.	S.W. by S.	213¾	S.33¾W.
N.E.	45	N.45E.	S.W.	225	S.45W.
N.E. by E.	56¼	N.56¼E.	S.W. by W.	236¼	S.56¼W.
E.N.E.	67½	N.67½E.	W.S.W.	247½	S.67½W.
E. by N.	78¾	N.78¾E.	W. by S.	258¾	S.78¾W.
E.	90	E.	W.	270	W.
E. by S.	101¼	S.78¾E.	W. by N.	281¼	N.78¾W.
E.S.E.	112½	S.67½E.	W.N.W.	292½	N.67½W.
S.E. by E.	123¾	S.56¼E.	N.W. by W.	303¾	N.56¼W.
S.E.	135	S.45E.	N.W.	315	N.45W.
S.E. by S.	146¼	S.33¾E.	N.W. by N.	326¼	N.33¾W.
S.S.E.	157½	S.22½E.	N.N.W.	337½	N.22½W.
S. by E.	168¾	S.11¼E.	N. by W.	348¾	N.11¼W.

EMERGENCY SIGNALS

THE DISTRESS SIGNAL used by everyone is S O S (short for "Save Our Souls"), made in Morse Code by any means available—radio, hooters and sirens, banging on drums, or even tapping on walls. The Morse Code for S O S is three dots, three dashes, three dots: ● ● ● ▬ ▬ ▬ ● ● ●

Ships

Apart from radio S O S, the following distress signals are made by ships:

In daylight: (i) a gun or other explosive signal fired at intervals of about a minute; (ii) the International Code flags N C; (iii) the "distant signal" consisting of a square flag having either above or below it a ball or anything resembling one; (iv) continuous sounding with any siren or fog-signalling apparatus.

In darkness: (i) the same as (i) above; (ii) flames on the vessel (as from a flare, a burning oil or tar barrel, a brazier filled with oil-soaked rags, etc.); (iii) rockets throwing stars of any colour fired at short intervals; (iv) as in (iv) above.

Emergency Ground Signals

When an aircraft has made a forced landing, the pilot of the grounded aircraft can signal to passing aircraft by means of the signals shown below. The shapes can be made of cloth, pieces of wood, stones, even trampled snow, and should be at least eight feet long.

Signal	Meaning	Signal	Meaning	Signal	Meaning
I	SERIOUS INJURIES SEND DOCTOR	¦	REQUIRE SIGNAL LAMP OR RADIO	L	REQUIRE FUEL AND OIL
II	SEND MEDICAL SUPPLIES	K	SHOW DIRECTION TO PROCEED	LL	ALL IS WELL
X	UNABLE TO PROCEED	↑	AM PROCEEDING THIS DIRECTION	N	NO
F	SEND FOOD AND WATER	I>	WILL ATTEMPT TAKE-OFF	Y	YES
≫	SEND FIREARMS AND AMMUNITION	L7	AIRCRAFT BADLY DAMAGED	JL	NOT UNDERSTOOD
□	SEND MAP AND COMPASS	△	PROBABLY SAFE TO LAND HERE	W	SEND ENGINEER

Aircraft in Distress

Apart from S O S given continuously by anything which will make sufficient noise (radio, siren, fog-horn, etc.) the pilot of an aircraft requiring urgent assistance can give any of the following signals: (i) The French words "M'aider" (pronounced "mayday") spoken continuously by radio telephony; (ii) red Very lights fired at short intervals; (iii) the International Code flags N C; (iv) the "distant signal" as for ships above.

MORSE CODE

THIS CODE was invented by Samuel Morse in 1872 for the purpose of sending messages by telegraph. Experienced Morse operators are able to tap out an average of 20 words (or 100 letters) a minute; automatic transmitters reach a speed of 40 to 50 words a minute.

The Code is made up of dots and dashes, a dash being three times the length of the dot. The time allowance between one symbol and the next is the length of a dot, between complete letters about two dots, and between words a dash.

Here is the complete Morse Code:

A	•—	J	•———	S	•••
B	—•••	K	—•—	T	—
C	—•—•	L	•—••	U	••—
D	—••	M	——	V	•••—
E	•	N	—•	W	•——
F	••—•	O	———	X	—••—
G	——•	P	•——•	Y	—•——
H	••••	Q	——•—	Z	——••
I	••	R	•—•		

Number	Code	Number	Code
1	•————	6	—••••
2	••———	7	——•••
3	•••——	8	———••
4	••••—	9	————•
5	•••••	0	—————

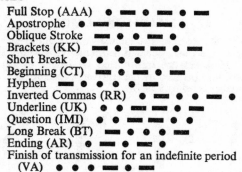

Full Stop (AAA)

Apostrophe

Oblique Stroke

Brackets (KK)

Short Break

Beginning (CT)

Hyphen

Inverted Commas (RR)

Underline (UK)

Question (IMI)

Long Break (BT)

Ending (AR)

Finish of transmission for an indefinite period
(VA)

(*Note:* CT is sent before each individual message, and is often repeated continuously for a stand-by signal; AR is sent to denote the end of a message but not the end of the transmission—the receiver still has to stand by until he gets the VA.)

Many people find it easier to learn the Code when they split the letters up into groups of similarities, as this:

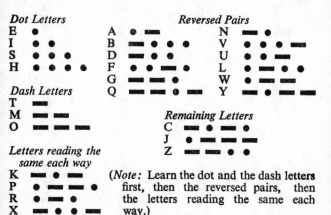

Dot Letters

E
I
S
H

Dash Letters

T
M
O

Letters reading the same each way

K
P
R
X

A
B
D
F
G
Q

Reversed Pairs

N
V
U
L
W
Y

Remaining Letters

C
J
Z

(*Note:* Learn the dot and the dash letters first, then the reversed pairs, then the letters reading the same each way.)

SEMAPHORE CODE

THIS CODE is used by two people within sight of each other, often by Scouts, Lifeboatmen, and ships within sight of shore. Messages are transmitted by means of two flags, their positions (as seen by the receiver) denoting the letters of the alphabet, as shown below.

Before a semaphore transmission begins, it is usual to hoist the letters VOX or simply J in International Code flags from a convenient flagstaff. The signaller then gives the Semaphore alphabetical sign, and waits until the person receiving the message replies with the letter C. If numbers are to be sent, the signaller makes the numeral sign; ne makes the alphabetical sign again when going back to ordinary letters.

When receiving, the signaller stands at the " ready " position, with the two flags crossed in front of the legs.

The Semaphore Code was invented in 1767, and was used for sending urgent messages across country from hill to hill before the invention of the telegraph.

INTERNATIONAL CODE

Forty flags of various colours and shapes are used to send messages in this Code, the flags being made up into hoists of two, three, or four at a time. Messages can be spelt out "in clear" with the Code, but this is very slow, and the flags are more frequently used in conjunction with a Code Book, various combinations of letters having special meanings (see *The International Code of Signals* published by H.M. Stationery Office).

Here are the Code flags, those marked "substitute" being used to repeat a flag already in a hoist.

THE INTERNATIONAL CODE FLAGS

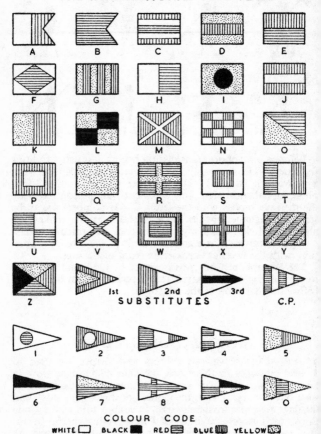

COLOUR CODE

WHITE ☐   BLACK ■   RED ▤   BLUE ▥   YELLOW ▨

The flags are made up of three colours plus black and white. The roped edge ("hoist") is assumed to be on the left in each case. (C.P.=Calling or Answering Pennant.)

Single flag hoists are sometimes made, and the meanings
of these when flown by ships are as follow:

A—Undergoing speed trials.
B—Explosives on board.
C—Yes.
D—Keep clear, I am in diffi-
   culties.
E—Altering course to star-
   board.
F—I am disabled.
G—Pilot wanted.
H—Pilot on board.
I—Altering course to port.
J—Sending message by sema-
   phore.
K—Stop at once.
L—Stop, I want to communi-
   cate with you.
M—A doctor is on board.
N—No.
O—Man overboard.
P—About to sail (the Blue
   Peter).
Q—Quarantine flag.
R—I have stopped.
S—Going astern.
T—Do not pass ahead of me.
U—You are in danger.
V—I need help.
W—Send a doctor.
X—Stop and watch for my
   signals.
Y—Carrying mails.
Z—Calling a shore station.

BRITISH LOCOMOTIVES

Locomotive Numbers

SINCE the nationalisation of the railways in Britain there
has been an extensive renumbering of locomotives along
the following lines:

Western Region (formerly G.W.R.): 1 to 9999.
Southern Region (formerly S.R.): All in the 30,000's
(steam—see overleaf for electric). The West Country class
begins 34 and the Merchant Navy class 35. The wartime
"Austerity" class starts 33.
Midland Region (formerly L.M.S.): 40,000 and 50,000
locos formerly numbered above 20,000 are now 58,000 and
upwards.
Eastern Region (formerly L.N.E.R.): All in the 60,000's.
North Eastern Region: see Eastern Region.
Scottish Region: see Midland and Eastern Regions accord-
ing to the former system referred to.
Special Locomotive Types: Diesel-electric locos have the
starting numbers 10,000, 12,000, 15,000, and diesel-mechanical

are 10,100 to 10,199 (Midland), and 11,000 upwards (Southern). Gas turbine locos, as they come into service, will have tne numbers 18,000 and up. Electric locos are from 20,000 to 29,999.

New standard types, 70,000 up.

Locomotive Liveries

Locomotives are generally painted in colours indicating the type of service to which they are allocated, as under:

Express Passenger: Dark green, lined black and orange.

Slow Passenger and Mixed Traffic: Black, lined cream, grey and red.

Freight: Plain black.

Main-line Diesels: Black with aluminium facings.

Locomotive Types

The present 400 different types of steam locomotives will eventually be replaced by about 12 types of standard design which will mostly have the following wheel arrangements: 2–6–0, 2–6–2 (Tank), 2–6–4 (Tank), 4–6–0, and 4–6–2.

Certain wheel arrangements bear special names, as under:

2–6–0	Mogul	2–8–2	Mikado
2–6–2	Prairie	4–4–2	Atlantic
2–6–4	Adriatic	4–6–2	Pacific
2–8–0	Consolidation	4–6–4	Baltic

Some Famous Locomotives

Mallard (Pacific type—Eastern no. 4468) holds the world speed record for steam locos at 126 m.p.h. (1938).

City of Bath (4–4–0—City class, Western no. 3433)—non-stop Paddington to Plymouth, nearly 246 miles, in 233½ minutes (1903).

Tregenna Castle (4–6–0—Castle class, Western no. 5006) —from Swindon to Paddington at average speed of 81·7 m.p.h. (1932).

Flying Scotsman (Pacific—Eastern no. 4472)—London to Leeds Central and back, touching 100 m.p.h. (1934).

Silver Link (4–6–2—streamlined Silver Jubilee class.

Eastern no. 2509, later renumbered 14) headed the first streamlined train in Britain, the "Silver Jubilee", London and Newcastle in 4 hours It touched 112½ m.p.h. in 1935.

Coronation (streamlined Pacific, 8P class, Midland no. 6220) touched 114 m.p.h. London to Crewe in 1937. She was the first of five in this class, the others being Queen Elizabeth (6221), Queen Mary (6222), Princess Alice (6223), and Princess Alexandra (6224).

King George V (4-6-0—King class, Western no. 6000) went to United States in 1927, and subsequently wore an American loco bell on her leading buffer beam.

Caerphilly Castle (4-6-0—Castle class, Western no. 4073) was the most powerful passenger loco in Britain when she was shown at the British Empire Exhibition, Wembley, in 1924.

Royal Scot (4-6-0—7P class, Midland no. 6100) was really the Royal Horse Guardsman renamed and renumbered when she went to North America and hauled the Royal Scot train over more than 11,000 miles of Canadian and American railroads in 1933.

The Princess Royal (Pacific—7P class, Midland no. 6200) was the first Pacific-type loco to be built for the old L.M.S.

Duchess of Hamilton (Pacific—streamlined 8P class, Midland no. 6229) was renamed and renumbered as Coronation (see above) for her trip to the United States with a Coronation Scot train in 1939. Owing to the outbreak of war, she was not returned to Britain until 1942.

Cock o' the North (Mikado—Eastern no. 2001) is a well-known London–Aberdeen loco. She belonged to Eastern class A2/2, which was subsequently converted to a 4-6-2 (Pacific) wheel arrangement.

Union of South Africa (Super-Pacific—class A4, Eastern no. 4488) was the first of the famous Dominion class, the others being Dominion of Canada (4489), Empire of India (4490), Commonwealth of Australia (4491), and Dominion of New Zealand (4492).   No. 4488 was given a South African loco whistle, and no. 4489 a C.P.R. whistle and bell.

(The numbers shown above are those given to the locomotives originally.   Present British Railway numbers are in accordance with the scheme described on page 131.)

AIRCRAFT REGISTRATION MARKS

A LL CIVIL aircraft must have a registration mark which must show clearly on the wings. In any registration mark, the first group of letters shows the country of origin; the second group indicates the identity of the aircraft. Thus: F—ABC means "Aircraft ABC of France". Marks of country of origin are given below.

AN	Nicaragua	OB	Peru
AP	Pakistan	OE	Austria
CB	Bolivia	OH	Finland
CC	Chile	OK	Czechoslovakia
CF	Canada	OO	Belgium
CN	Morocco	OY	Denmark
CR	Portuguese Colonies	PH	Netherlands
CS	Portugal	PI	Philippine Islands
CU	Cuba	PJ	Netherlands West
CX	Uruguay		Indies
EC	Spain	PK	Indonesia, Republic
EI	Eire		of
EP	Persia	PP	Brazil
ET	Ethiopia	PT	Brazil
F	France	PZ	Surinam
G	Great Britain and	RX	Panama
	Northern Ireland	SA	Saudi Arabia
HA	Hungary	SE	Sweden
HB	Switzerland	SN	The Sudan
HC	Ecuador	SP	Poland
HH	Haiti	SR	Syria
HI	Dominica	SU	Egypt
HK	Colombia	SX	Greece
HS	Thailand	TC	Turkey
I	Italy	TF	Iceland
LG	Guatemala	TI	Costa Rica
LI	Liberia	VH	Australia
LN	Norway	VO	Newfoundland
LR	Lebanon	VPA	Ashanti, Gold Coast
LV	Argentina	VPB	Bahamas
LX	Luxembourg	VPC	Ceylon
LZ	Bulgaria	VPF	Falkland Islands
MC	Monte Carlo	VPG	British Guiana
N	United States	VPH	British Honduras
NX	United States (Experi-	VPJ	Jamaica
	mental)	VPK	Kenya

VPM	Malta		VRN	Nigeria and British
VPN	Nyasaland			Cameroons
VPP	Western Pacific		VRR	Malaya
	Islands		VRS	Malaya
VPR	Northern Rhodesia		VRT	Tanganyika
VPS	British Somaliland		VRU	British North Borneo
VPT	Trinidad and Tobago		VT	India
VPU	Uganda		XA	Mexico
VPV	St. Vincent		XB	Mexico
VPX	Gambia		XH	Honduras
VPY	Southern Rhodesia		XT	China
VPZ	Zanzibar		XY	Burma
VQB	Barbados		YA	Afghanistan
VQC	Cyprus		YI	Iraq
VQF	Fiji Islands		YJ	New Hebrides
VQG	Grenada		YR	Rumania
VQH	St. Helena		YS	Salvador
VQL	St. Lucia		YU	Yugoslavia
VQM	Mauritius		YV	Venezuela
VQP	Palestine		ZA	Albania
VQS	Seychelle Islands		ZK	New Zealand
VRB	Bermuda		ZP	Paraguay
VRG	Gibraltar		ZS	Union of South
VRH	Hong Kong			Africa
VRL	Sierra Leone		4X	Israel

NOTES ON WOODWORKING

Woods to Use

FOR MODEL AEROPLANES use *balsa*. It is very light (only about half the weight of cork), nearly white, and quite pliable. It can be bought at model-shops in square and rectangular sections of various sizes and lengths. Joins are best made with balsa cement.

For rough work (tool racks, rabbit hutches, etc.) use *pine* for framing and *plywood* for panels. Pine (often called "deal") is nearly white, fairly strong, and quite easy to work. It is the wood used for house timbers—roofing, floors, joists, window-frames, and so on. Plywood is made up of thin layers of wood glued together, and it can often be bought with the top layer of some expensive wood. Five- and seven-ply are the best for strength; three-ply is thin and should not be used where the panels are to be large.

For work benches, tables, etc. which have to be scrubbed now and then to get them clean, use *spruce*. It is fairly soft, easy to work, and comes up like new when well washed.

For outdoor work such as gates and fences use *larch*. It is heavier and harder than pine, and has a warm red appearance.

For better work (furniture, for example) the *hardwoods* are best, although they are expensive, difficult to work, and need constantly sharpened tools. The usual home-grown hardwoods are elm (specially good for underwater parts, as in boat-building), oak, sycamore, walnut, and ash.

For all outdoor work it is best to coat any wood with creosote to retard the onset of rot.

Screws and Screw-holes

The diameters of screws are given in numbers, from 0000 to 50, the last being the largest. Each diameter can be bought in different lengths according to the thickness of the work to be screwed.

For light work the usual sizes are 3, 4, 6 and 8. Below is a table showing the sizes of holes to be drilled for clearance and for the threads to cut into.

Screw size	Clearance hole (in.)	Thread hole (in.)
3	$\frac{7}{64}$	$\frac{1}{16}$
4	$\frac{1}{8}$	$\frac{5}{64}$
6	$\frac{5}{32}$	$\frac{5}{64}$
8	$\frac{3}{16}$	$\frac{3}{32}$

Screws can be bought with three kinds of heads: countersunk, raised, and round. Where the screw has to be level with the wood when driven in, countersunk screws must be used. Raised heads look decorative; round heads should always be used with washers under them.

Furniture Sizes

Chairs: Height of seat from ground, 18 in.; width of seat. 18 in.; depth of seat (front to back), 16 in.

Tables: Height of top from ground, 30 in. The most useful sizes of table-tops are—36 in. by 36 in., 36 in. by 42 in., and 36 in. by 48 in.

Writing Tables: These are slightly lower than ordinary tables—27 to 28 in. is a good height. A useful size for a small one is 24 in. by 30 in.

Bookcases: Most books are from 7 in. to 10¼ in. high, and a four-shelf bookcase should be arranged so that the top shelf is 7¼ in. high, the next 8 in., the third 9 in., and the fourth 10½ in. This makes a total height, allowing for thickness of wood, of nearly 30 in. The shelves should be 7 in. deep (from front to back), and a good width for a bookcase is 24 to 30 in. The timber used should be strong—say ¾ in. thick.

For more information, read *Woodworker's Pocket Book*, Charles H. Hayward (Evans).

NOTES ON METAL-WORKING

Metals to Use

NEARLY ALL metal-working at home is done with sheet-metal, which can be bought in various sizes up to about 24 in. by 48 in. and in various gauges. The gauges are based upon the Standard Wire Gauge, and below is a table showing the most useful thicknesses for model work and general home use.

S.W.G.	Thickness (in.)	S.W.G.	Thickness (in.)
16	0·064	22	0·028
18	0·048	24	0·022
20	0·036	26	0·018

When ordering sheet-metal, you would ask for the size you want, and give the thickness as, say, "18 S.W.G.".

Sheet-metal is made in the following:

Aluminium: a very soft metal, easy to bend and drill, and does not tarnish easily. Cannot be soldered by ordinary home means.

Aluminium Alloys (Dural, Birmabright, Alclad, etc.): these are stronger than aluminium, but a little harder to work. Dural is nearly as strong as mild steel, but it is difficult to bend without complicated heat-treatment. Cannot be soldered.

Brass: the almost perfect sheet-metal—it can be bent,

drilled, cut, and soldered. Before bending, it must be annealed; that is, heated to dull red and plunged into cold water.

Copper not so strong as brass, but very easy to work. Needs annealing before bending. Will take solder well.

Tin Plate: this is mild steel coated with tin to prevent rust. It can be bent, drilled, cut, and soldered without much trouble.

Screws and Screw-holes

Screw diameters are stated in numbers to standards set by the British Association (B.A.) and other bodies. The most useful diameters for home use are 8B.A., 6B.A., 4B.A., and 2B.A., the last being the largest. Screws of the various diameters can be bought in various lengths, together with nuts to fit them. The length of screw should be the thickness of the pieces of work to be bolted together, plus enough for the nut.

The sizes of drills for making holes to take B.A. screws are as follow: 8B.A., $\frac{3}{32}$ in.; 6B.A., $\frac{1}{8}$ in.; 4B.A., $\frac{5}{32}$ in.; and 2B.A., $\frac{3}{16}$ in.

Lathe Speeds

When using a lathe, the speed at which the surface of the work should be fed to the cutting tool is shown below. Some metals are turned dry, but others have to have lubricant poured over them during cutting. The lubricant required in any particular case is also shown below.

Metal	Turning Speed (in. per sec.)	Lubricant
Aluminium	20–30	Paraffin
Dural	40–50	Paraffin
Brass	20–25	(Turn dry)
Copper	20–30	(Turn dry)
Mild steel	12–15	Thin oil

To find out at what speed the spindle of the lathe should turn, use the following formula: $s = \pi d$, where s = the speed of the spindle in revs. per second, d = diameter of work in inches, and $\pi = 3 \cdot 1416$ or $\frac{22}{7}$.

Bending Allowances

When bending sheet-metal, extra allowance has to be made for the metal taken up by the bend, or the work will be too small when it is finished. Below are the allowances to be made for bending various gauges to right angles.

S.W.G. of Metal	Bending Allowances		
	$\frac{1}{32}$ in. rad.	$\frac{1}{16}$ in. rad.	$\frac{1}{8}$ in. rad.
16	0·1	0·125	0·25
18	0·075	0·13	0·225
20	0·07	0·12	0·22
22	0·065	0·115	0·2
24	0·06	0·11	0·2
26	0·055	0·1	0·2

Since these bending allowances will be difficult to measure, it is best to cut metal which has to be bent to $\frac{1}{16}$ in. or $\frac{1}{8}$ in. larger than required without the bend, then after bending file the edges until an exact fit is obtained.

Tempering Data

To harden tools, heat the whole length of the blade to a medium red and plunge into lukewarm water. The metal is now very brittle and must be tempered.

To temper, reheat near to the cutting edge gently until one of the colours shown below is seen on the surface of the metal at the edge, then plunge again into lukewarm water. The tool can now be sharpened on an oilstone if required, and is ready for use.

Tempering Colour	Suitable for
Light straw	Scribers, dividers, lathe tools for brass, scrapers, hammer faces.
Dark straw	Drills.
Dark yellow	Cutting shears, boring cutters, chisels for steel, penknives.
Light purple	Punches, razor-edge knives (lino cutters, etc.).
Dark purple	Chisels for cast iron.
Pale blue	Needles, screwdrivers.
Dark blue	Saws for wood, springs.

MIXING COLOURS

(For Oil Paints, Water Colours and Inks)

(Note: Quantities of each colour are not given because the various component colours have to be experimented with to give the exact shade required.)

To get	*Mix together*
Buff	Yellow, White, and a little Venetian Red.
Chestnut	Chrome Yellow and Venetian Red.
Chocolate	Burnt Sienna and Carmine
Cream	Yellow Ochre and White.
Fawn	Yellow Ochre, Burnt Umber, and White.
Flesh	Yellow Ochre, Burnt Sienna, and White.
French Grey	Prussian Blue, White, and a little Crimson Lake.
Gold	Chrome Yellow and a small quantity of White and Vermilion.
Grey (Leaden)	Black and White.
Lavender	Ultramarine, Madder Lake, and White.
Lemon	Chrome Yellow and White
Mahogany	Orange Chrome (see Orange below), Burnt Sienna, and a little White.
Maroon	Venetian Red, Indian Red, and a little Black.
Oak	Yellow Ochre, Burnt Umber, and White
Olive Green	Prussian Blue and Raw Umber
Orange	Chrome Yellow and Vermilion.
Peach	Vermilion and White.
Pea Green	Prussian Blue, White, and a little Chrome Yellow.
Pearl Grey	White with a little Prussian Blue and Black.
Pink	Carmine and White.
Purple	Ultramarine, Crimson Lake, and a little White.
Rose	Crimson Lake and White.
Sage Green	Prussian Blue, Raw Umber, and a little White.
Salmon	Venetian Red and White.
Silver Grey	Indigo and a little Black.
Sky Blue	Prussian Blue, White, and a little Crimson Lake.

Stone	Yellow Ochre, White, and a little Burnt Umber
Violet	Indigo, Vermilion, and White.
Walnut	Burnt Umber and Raw Sienna.

PHOTOGRAPHIC TABLES AND FORMULÆ

Exposure Table (Fast Films)

In this table, columns marked "1" are for cameras with variable diaphragms (folding cameras mostly) and the shutter is set to 1/50th second; columns marked "2" are for box cameras with two stop-openings (Small and Large) and with the shutter set for Instantaneous (I) or Snapshot (S).

Scene	Bright Sun		Hazy Sun		Cloudy Bright	
	1	2	1	2	1	2
Beach Scenes, Snow Scenes, Distant Landscapes	f.32	Small	f.22	Small	f.16	Large
Medium Landscapes	f.22	Small	f.16	Large	f.11	—
Close Landscapes, Streets, Groups of People	f.16	Small	f.11	Large	f.8	—
Portraits, Shady Scenes	f.11	Large	f.8	Large	f.5·6	—

(*Note:* With exposures marked in columns 1, the photograph should be taken some time between two hours after sunrise and two hours before sunset; for column 2 exposures, three hours after sunrise and three hours before sunset.)

Stop Factors

To calculate the correct exposure for any stop, find out the proper exposure for f.8, and multiply by the factors given below:

$$\textit{when } f.8 \text{ (or } f.7.7) = 1$$

$f.11$ (or $f.11·3$) = 2	$f.5·6$ (or $f.6·3$) = $\frac{1}{2}$
$f.16$ = 3	$f.4$ (or $f.4·5$) = $\frac{1}{4}$
$f.22$ = 4	$f.2·8$ (or $f.3·5$) = $\frac{1}{8}$

Film and Plate Sizes

Film or Plate Size	*No. Pictures on Film*	*Size of Pictures Inches*	*Equiv. Metric*
35 mm.	36	1 × 1½	24 mm. × 36 mm.
B.27 or 127	16	1⅛ × 1¾	4 cm. × 3 cm.
„	12	1¾ × 1¾	4 cm. × 4 cm.
„ (Vest-pocket)	8	2½ × 1¾	4·5 cm. × 6 cm.
B.20, 120 or 620	16	2¼ × 1⅝	4·5 cm. × 6 cm.
„	12	2¼ × 2¼	6 cm. × 6 cm.
„	8	2¼ × 3¼	6 cm. × 9 cm.
Lantern	(Plate)	3¼ × 3¼	9 cm. × 9 cm.
Quarter-plate	6	4¼ × 3¼	12 cm. × 9 cm.
Postcard	6	5½ × 3½	
Half-plate	(Plate)	6½ × 4¾	
Whole-plate	(Plate)	8½ × 6½	

(*Note:* For special purposes, larger sizes of plates are obtainable—10 in. × 8 in.; 12 in. × 10 in.; 15 in. × 12 in.; 20 in. × 16 in.; and 30 in. × 20 in.)

Film and Plate Developers

M-Q (Metol-Hydroquinone) Developer

Water	20 ounces	500 c.c.
Metol	20 grains	1 grm.
Sodium sulphite (cryst.)	3 ounces	75 grm.
Hydroquinone	80 grains	4 grm.
Sodium carbonate (cryst.)	2 ounces	50 grm.
Potassium bromide	20 grains	1 grm.

(Dissolve the chemicals in the order given.)

For dish development, use 1 part of the above to 2 parts of water, and develop for 5 min. if Orthochromatic or ordinary Panchromatic emulsion, and for only 3½ min. if Fine-grain Pan.

Fine-grain Developer

Water	20 ounces	500 c.c.
Sodium sulphite (cryst.)	4 ounces	100 grm.
Hydroquinone	50 grains	2·5 grm.
Borax	20 grains	1 grm.

(Dissolve the chemicals in the order given.)

This developer is used as mixed, and the time of development is from 12 to 20 min., the shorter time for fine-grain emulsions, the longer time for ordinary emulsions.

Printing Paper Developers

For nearly all papers (gaslight, bromide, and chlorobromide), the M-Q Developer given above will be suitable. Use the Developer with only 1 part of water for gaslight, 2 parts of water for the others.

A special paper-developer can be made up as follows:

Amidol Developer

Water	20 ounces	500 c.c.
Sodium sulphite (cryst.)	240 grains	27·5 grm.
Potassium bromide	6 grains	0·8 grm.
Amidol	24 grains	2·75 grm.

(Dissolve the chemicals in the order given.)

For bromide papers, develop for 2 min.; for gaslight papers, develop for 45 sec. This developer cannot be stored, and should not be kept longer than 24 hours.

Fixing Baths

Ordinary Fixing Bath

Water	20 ounces	500 c.c.
Sodium thiosulphate (hypo)	5 ounces	125 grm.

Acid Fixing Bath

Water	20 ounces	500 c.c.
Hypo	5 ounces	125 grm.
Potassium metabisulphite	½ ounce	12·5 grm.

(To make an acid fixing and hardening bath, add chrome alum, ¼ oz.)

For more information, read *Photographer's Pocket Book* or *Enjoy Your Photography*, Carlton Wallace (Evans).

BROADCASTING

ALLOCATIONS of radio air-space for broadcasting (sound only, and television plus sound) consist of a number of wavebands (sound only) and frequency bands (television, and frequency-modulated sound), as follow:

Long Waves (sound)	700 to 2,000 metres
Medium Waves (sound)	195 to 600 metres

Short Waves (sound)	15 to 65 metres
Band I (television)	41 to 68 mc/s
Band II (FM/VHF sound)	87·5 to 100 mc/s
Band III (television)	174 to 216 mc/s
Band IV (not in use yet)	470 to 585 mc/s
Band V (not in use yet)	610 to 960 mc/s

mc/s=megacycles per second (see below)

For radio communication generally, and for such purposes as radar and radio control, there are two other ways of grouping radio waves—by extended Wavebands, and by Frequency Bands. Radio Waves are measured in Metres; Frequencies are measured in Kilocycles and Megacycles (1 mc. = 1,000 kc.) per second.

For the formula to convert metres to kc/s. see page 113.

The names of the new Wavebands are:

Myriametric	10,000 metres and over
Kilometric (Long)	10,000 to 1,000 metres
Hectometric (Medium)	1,000 to 100 metres
Decametric (Short)	100 to 10 metres
Metric	10 metres to 1 metre
Decimetric	1 metre to 10 centimetres
Centimetric (also called "microwaves")	10 centimetres to 1 centimetre

The names of the new Frequency Bands are:

Very Low Frequency (VLF)	30 Kc/s. and less
Low Frequency (LF)	30 to 300 Kc/s.
Medium Frequency (MF)	300 Kc/s. to 3 Mc/s.
High Frequency (HF)	3 to 30 Mc/s.
Very High Frequency (VHF)	30 to 300 Mc/s.
Ultra High Frequency (UHF)	300 to 3,000 Mc/s.
Super High Frequency (SHF)	3,000 to 30,000 Mc/s.

Medium and Short Wavebands

Medium Waves are the easiest to receive on ordinary radio sets, and are used for national and regional broadcasting.

Short Waves travel very great distances, but are likely to "fade" at times. Here are hints for receiving short-wave transmissions: around 16 metres, when both transmitter and receiver are in daylight; 19 metres, when both are in twilight;

25 metres, when the transmitter is in daylight and the receiver is in darkness; 31 metres, when the transmitter is in darkness and the receiver is in daylight; 49 metres, when both are in darkness.

When searching for overseas short-wave stations, try the following times and wavelengths: *Europe*, daytime 16 metres, evening 25 metres, and 49 metres; *Canada and America*, afternoon 16 metres, twilight 19 metres, evening 25 metres; *Australia and Far East*, sunrise to noon, 31 metres.

PRINCIPAL BROADCAST TRANSMITTERS

IN APRIL, 1950, changes were made in the wavelengths of many Long and Medium Wave broadcasting stations which can normally be received in Britain; the changes were made by an international agreement known as the Copenhagen Plan.

The new wavelengths are included in the list below.

Wavelength (metres)	Station	Power (Kilowatts)
Long Wave		
1829	Allouis (France)	250
1734	Moscow (U.S.S.R.)	500
1571	Motala (Sweden)	200
1500	Droitwich (England)	400
1376	Oslo (Norway)	100
1224	Kalundborg (Denmark)	150
Medium Wave		
567	Beromünster (Switzerland)	150
530	Athlone (Eire)	100
506	Sundsvall (Sweden)	150
484	Brussels (Belgium)	150
470	Prague (Czechoslovakia)	120
464	Droitwich (England)	120
433	Moorside Edge (England)	150

Wavelength (metres)	Station	Power (Kilowatts)
422	Marseilles (France)	150
402	Hilversum (Netherlands)	120
393	Sottens (Switzerland)	150
388	Stockholm (Sweden)	55
379	Limoges (France)	100
371	Westerglen (Scotland)	100
359	Nancy (France)	150
355	Rome (Italy)	100
348	Paris (France)	100
344	Moscow (U.S.S.R.)	150
340	Washford (Wales)	150
334	Milan (Italy)	50
330	Brookman's Park (England)	150
324	Brussels (Belgium)	20
318	Toulouse (France)	100
309	Hamburg (Germany)	50

303	Berlin (Germany)	100
298	Hilversum (Netherlands)	120
285	Start Point (England)	150
276	Droitwich (England)	150
261	Lisnagarvey (N. Ireland)	100
259	Strasbourg (France)	20
251	Munich (Germany)	100
249	Bordeaux (France)	100
247	Brookman's Park (England)	60

245	Falun (Sweden)	100
240	Dublin (Ireland)	5
228	Stavanger (Norway)	100
224	Crowborough (England)	150
218	Lille (France)	20
208	Luxembourg (Luxembourg)	150
205	Monte Carlo (Monaco)	150
196	Vatican City (Vatican State)	100

Short Waves

Short-wave stations are so close together on the tuning dial that they are best considered as grouped together in bands (see *Short-Wave Bands* on page 144), and identified by listening for their call-signs. Below are listed some of the more powerful short-wave broadcast transmitters and their call-signs within or very near to the bands named, given in high-to-low wavelength order in each band.

49-metre band: Lima (Peru), OAX4Z; Tokio (Japan), JLR; Boston (U.S.A.), WRUS; New York (U.S.A.), WCBN; Cincinnati (U.S.A.), WLWK; Sackville (Canada, CKOB; Sao Paulo (Brazil), ZYB7; New York (U.S.A.), WNRX; San Francisco (U.S.A.), KNBI; Leopoldville (Belgian Congo), OQ2AA; Delhi (India), VUD10.

31-metre band: Ankara (Turkey), TAP; Mexico City (Mexico), XEWW; Colon (Panama), HOLA; Schenectady (U.S.A.), WGEO; Shepparton (Australia), VLB; San Francisco (U.S.A.), KWID; Sackville (Canada), CHLS; Montevideo (Uruguay), CXA6; Honolulu (Hawaii), KRHO; New York (U.S.A.), WNRX; Rio de Janeiro (Brazil), PRL7.

25-metre band: Leopoldville (Belgian Congo), OTC3; Cincinnati (U.S.A.), WLWR1; Shepparton (Australia), VLB10; Schenectady (U.S.A.), WGEA; San Francisco (U.S.A.), KWID.

19-metre band: Colombo (Ceylon), announces as "Colombo"; Delhi (India), VUD7; Shepparton (Australia), VLA6; San Francisco (U.S.A.), KGEX; Cincinnati (U.S.A.),

WLWR; Schenectady (U.S.A.), WGEO; Brazzaville (French East Africa), FZI.

16-*metre band:* Wellington (New Zealand), ZL5; New York (U.S.A.), WNBI; Shepparton (Australia), VLA7; Sackville (Canada), CKNC; Rio de Janeiro (Brazil), PRL9.

ROAD SIGNALS

IT is important when cycling to give other road-users very clear indications of one's intentions. Below are signals which should be made by every cyclist.

I am going to turn to the—

left

right

I am slowing down
or stopping

Please over-
take me

In addition, all road-users should know the meaning of road signs. Some of these signs are shown overleaf.

ROAD SIGNS

The eleven signs above are warnings of road conditions ahead.

The signs marked HALT, SLOW and 30 (the beginning of a 30 m.p.h. speed limit) must be obeyed by all road-users. The fourth sign marks the end of a speed-limit.

HIKING AND CAMPING REMINDERS

Notes on Packing

WHEN packing, roll blanket or sleeping bag in groundsheet for strapping to the back of the belt. Place spare clothing (except socks) at the bottom of the large partition in the rucksack; put socks in one of the small pockets so that they can be got at easily.

Some cooking equipment can be strapped to the back of the rucksack on the outside. The tent in its valise (it should be very light unless a bicycle is being taken) can be strapped on top of the rucksack if there is no room for it inside.

Hiking

The list below will remind you of what to pack if you are staying at hostels overnight and eating in cafés.

If you intend to eat on the march, then you will also require the items shown under *Cooking and Eating* in the Camping list.

Clothing	Brush and comb
Swim suit	Mirror (metal)
Spare shirt	Foot ointment
,, shorts	
,, socks	*Equipment, etc.*
,, handkerchiefs	Rucksack
,, shoe-laces	Jack-knife
	Map
Toilet Requisites	Pocket compass
Soap and towel	Water bottle
Toothbrush	Money
Toothpaste	P.O. Savings Book

Camping

All the above, and in addition:

Camp Equipment	*Cooking and Eating*
Tent with pegs in valise	Cooking stove
Spare pegs	Fuel for above
Hank of cord	Matches
Groundsheet	Canteen or billycan
Blanket or sleeping bag	Knife, fork, spoon
Rubber pillow	Plate and mug
Canvas bucket	Sandwich tin (for tea, sugar, etc.)
Candle lantern or electric	Butter muslin (for covering food)
torch	Tin and bottle opener

Hikers' and Campers' Code

1. Always ask permission before cooking or camping on private ground.

2. If told that you are trespassing, apologise and leave at once.

3. Close all gates behind you, and take care not to damage fences or hedges if climbing over them.

4. Always light fires on a patch of dry, barren ground, and never in grass or woodland or close to hedges and haystacks.

5. Stamp out all fires before you move on.

6. When attending to the wants of nature, keep a good distance from streams, ponds, and wells. Use low-lying ground, and bury any solid material deeply. (Ask permission to use a W.C. whenever possible.)

7. When washing up, draw water from a stream and wash up well away from its banks. Scatter the dirty water on dry ground afterwards.

8. When breaking camp, bury all rubbish and tidy up before you leave.

ANIMAL AND BIRD TRACKS

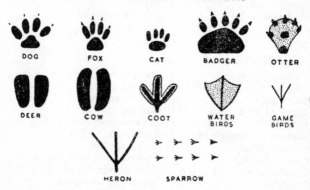

These tracks are most likely to be found in soft soil, in dust or in thick mud (wet or dried) in the country. Dotted tracks indicate animals or birds who swim. The sparrow track is characteristic of those made by all hopping birds.

PETS' FEEDING DATA

Dogs

T HE TABLE below applies to puppies from the age of 7 to
8 weeks. The tiny pets should be fed according to
body-weight (easily found out on a pair of household scales),
and the owner should remember that overfeeding is as un-
kind as underfeeding, for it causes all kinds of stomach and
other troubles.

Weight of Dog	Food per day	Weight of Dog	Food per day
1 lb.	2½ oz.	15 lb.	16 oz.
2 lb.	3½ oz.	20 lb.	1¼ lb.
3 lb.	5 oz.	25 lb.	1½ lb.
4 lb.	6 oz.	30 lb.	1¾ lb.
6 lb.	7½ oz.	50 lb.	2½ lb.
8 lb.	10 oz.	75 lb.	3¼ lb.
10 lb.	12½ oz.	100 lb.	4 lb.

(The above table is taken from *Boy's Book of Hobbies*)

Up to 4 months old, feed four times daily; from 4 to 6
months, three times daily; from 6 to 12 months, twice daily;
above 12 months, once daily.

Cats

Kittens will be fed by their mother up to about 7 or 8
weeks of age, after which the rule should be about ½ oz.
of solid food per day for each pound of body-weight, plus
some milk. Cats generally forage for themselves to a great
extent, hunting mice, birds, and so on. They also like to
eat a little fresh grass now and then, so they should have
access to a lawn or strip of grassland.

YOUTH ORGANISATIONS

Air Training Corps is a voluntary organisation which gives
training to boys 13–18 who want to go in for flying (R.A.F.
or Civil) as a career. The training includes ground duties,
navigation, airframes and engines, aircraft recognition,
flights in service aircraft (powered and gliders), and radio,

there is also plenty of sport and an active club life. **Local** headquarters: any R.A.F. station or recuiting depot.

Army Cadet Force gives training in leadership to boys who are interested in the Regular or Territorial Armies. There are units in every part of Britain. The training includes field-craft, drill, and map reading, and all cadets get opportunities to attend summer camps and to learn to shoot. Cadet units provide games and club activities for their members. Headquarters: 16, Buckingham Palace Road, London, S.W.1.

Boys' Brigade is an organisation which gives training in gymnastics, ambulance work, scouting, athletics, swimming, and sports generally. It holds Summer camps and organises many boys' clubs. It is divided into companies, each of which is connected with a church or other Christian organisation. Ages: 12 to 18. Headquarters: Abbey House, Westminster, London, S.W.1.

Boy Scouts welcomes boys of any age who are interested in an outdoor life—tracking and stalking, camping, reconnoitring, cooking, first aid, signalling, and sport. There are some 5 million Scouts in the world, half a million of whom are in Britain. Headquarters: 25, Buckingham Palace Road, London, S.W.1.

Camping Club of Great Britain and Ireland provides facilities for camping and caravanning, canoeing and mountaineering, organises rallies, and provides lists of camping sites. Headquarters: 38, Grosvenor Gardens, London, S.W.1.

Combined Cadet Force is the cadet organisation in schools which keep boys up to age 18. Every contingent has a basic section where preliminary training is given. Schools have one or more advanced Service Sections (R.N., Army, R.A.F.), and members of each section wear the uniform of their Service. C.C.F. Cadets attend annual camp with their parent Services. Headquarters: 16, Buckingham Palace Road, London, S.W.1.

Cyclists' Touring Club is the organisation which looks after the cyclist on the road. It issues a handbook, maps, and itineraries, inspects and recommends hostels, and provides free third-party insurance to its members. It also organises tours and social events. Headquarters: 3, Craven Hill, London, W.2.

National Federation of Young Farmers' Clubs organises and gives help to some 1,240 Young Farmers' Clubs throughout Britain, arranging meetings and social events and advising upon agricultural education. Headquarters: 55, Gower Street, London, W.C.1.

National Union of Students organises inexpensive educational tours abroad, harvest camps, an international student and correspondence exchange, and a hostel in London. It also advises upon scholarships and grants, hostels, recreation facilities, and anything of value to the young student. Headquarters: 3, Endsleigh Street, London, W.C.1.

Ramblers' Association arranges group visits to places of historical interest and natural beauty, and looks after the interests of ramblers generally. Headquarters: 48, Park Road, Baker Street, London, N.W.1.

Sea Cadet Corps provides training for boys between 12 and 18 who are thinking of entering the Royal Navy or Merchant Navy as a career. There are 375 units in Britain, controlled jointly by the Admiralty and the Navy League, and each unit gives its members facilities for making short voyages and working small ships. Headquarters: Grand Buildings, Trafalgar Square, London, W.C.2.

Young Men's Christian Association (Y.M.C.A.) provides clubs, libraries, rooms for lectures and recreation, gymnasiums and hostels to all who are interested in the development of the Christian character. It is a world-wide organisation with some 376 local associations in Britain and nearly 6,000 abroad. Headquarters: 112, Great Russell Street, London, W.C.1.

Youth Hostels Association controls inexpensive hostels throughout Britain for the use of all who love the countryside. At the hostels, members may either buy meals cheaply, or cook their own. Nearly all the hostels are situated in beauty spots or other holiday centres. Headquarters: Trevelyan House, St. Albans, Herts; 7 Bruntsfield Crescent, Edinburgh 10.

SPORTS RECORDS

ATHLETICS AND SWIMMING

World Records

Event Running	Latest Holders	Time min. sec.	Speed m.p.h.
100 yards	9 holders (8 U.S.A., 1 Australian)	9·3	22·00
100 metres	4 holders (all U.S.A.)	10·1	22·16
220 yards	D. Sime (U.S.A.)	20·0	22·50
200 metres	D. Sime (U.S.A.)	20·0	22·30
440 yards	G. A. Davis (U.S.A.)	45·7	19·68
400 metres	L. Jones (U.S.A.)	45·2	19·80
880 yards	T. Courtney (U.S.A.)	1 46·8	16·86
800 metres	R. Moens (Belgium)	1 45·7	16·94
1 mile	H. J. Elliott (Australia)	3 54·5	15·33
1,500 metres	H. J. Elliott (Australia)	3 36·0	15·53
2,000 metres	I. Rozsavolgyi (Hungary)	5 02·2	14·81
3,000 metres	G. Pirie (Gt. Britain)	7 52·8	14·19
3 miles	A. G. Thomas (Australia)	13 10·8	13·66
5,000 metres	V. Kuts (U.S.S.R.)	13 35·0	13·72

Hurdling			
120 yards	J. Davis (U.S.A.)	13·4	18·32
110 metres	J. Davis (U.S.A.)	13·4	18·37
220 yards	E. Gilbert (U.S.A.)	22·1	20·36
200 metres	D. Sime (U.S.A.)	22·2	20·16
440 yards	G. C. Potgieter (S. Africa)	49·7	18·10
400 metres	G. Davis (U.S.A.)	49·2	18·18

Swimming (Free Style)			
100 metres	J. Devitt (Australia)	54·6	4·10
200 metres	J. Konrads (Australia)	2 03·2	3·63
400 metres	J. Konrads (Australia)	4 21·8	3·42
800 metres	J. Konrads (Australia)	9 14·5	3·24
1,500 metres	J. Konrads (Australia)	17 28·7	3·20

Other Events

Long Jump	J. C. Owens (U.S.A.)	26 ft.	8¼ in.
High Jump	Y. Stepanov (U.S.S.R.)	7 ft.	1 in.
Pole Vault	R. A. Gutowski (U.S.A.)	15 ft.	8½ in.
Discus	F. Gordien (U.S.A.)	194 ft.	6 in.
Hammer	H. V. Connolly (U.S.A.)	225 ft.	4 in.
Javelin	E. Danielsen (Norway)	281 ft.	2 in.
Weight	W. P. O'Brien (U.S.A.)	63 ft.	2 in.

Records Within Britain

Event	Latest Holders	Details

Running

100 yards	P. F. Radford (Gt. Britain) +3 others	9·6 sec.
220 yards	E. B. Jeffery (S. Africa) +2 others	20·9 sec.
440 yards	M. Singh (India)	46·6 sec.
880 yards	H. J. Elliott (Australia)	1 min. 47·3 sec.
1 mile	H. J. Elliott (Australia)	3 min. 55·6 sec.
3 miles	M. G. Halberg (N. Zealand)	13 min. 15·0 sec.

Hurdling

120 yards	H. Dillard (U.S.A.)	13·9 sec.
220 yards	P. B. Hildreth (Gt. Britain)	23·3 sec.
440 yards	G. C. Potgieter (S. Africa)	49·7 sec.

Swimming

100 yards	G. Larsson (Sweden)	51·0 sec.
150 yards	J. I. Hale (Gt. Britain)	1 min. 26·3 sec.
220 yards	J. C. Waldrop (Gt. Britain)	2 min. 10·0 sec.
300 yards	J. I. Hale (Gt. Britain)	3 min. 12·3 sec.
440 yards	J. C. Waldrop (Gt. Britain)	4 min. 41·9 sec.
500 yards	J. I. Hale (Gt. Britain)	5 min. 46·8 sec.
880 yards	J. C. Waldrop (Gt. Britain)	10 min. 3·6 sec.

Other Events

Long Jump	W. Steele (U.S.A.)	25 ft.	8 in.
High Jump	2 U.S.S.R. holders	6 ft.	11¼ in.
Pole Vault	D. G. Bragg (U.S.A.)	15 ft.	0 in.

Discus	K. Merta (Czechoslovakia)	186 ft.	0	in.
Hammer	M. Krivonosov (U.S.S.R.)	212 ft.	6	in.
Javelin	V. Kuznetsov (U.S.S.R.)	271 ft.	11½	in.
Weight	A. Rowe (Gt. Britain)	58 ft.	11	in.

UNIVERSITY BOAT RACE

THE RACE is rowed at the end of March or the beginning of April in each year from Putney to Mortlake, a distance of nearly 4¼ miles. The time of the race is at flood tide, one hour before it turns.

The first race was in 1856. During the war 6 years 1940 to 1945 there were no official races, but meetings were held unofficially at various places.

From 1945 the race was rowed on the Putney–Mortlake course. The following are the last ten results:

Year	Winner	By	Time
1949	Cambridge	¼ length	18 min. 57 sec.
1950	Cambridge	3½ lengths	20 min. 15 sec.
1951	Cambridge	12 lengths	20 min. 50 sec.
1952	Oxford	A few feet	20 min. 23 sec.
1953	Cambridge	8 lengths	19 min. 54 sec.
1954	Oxford	4¼ lengths	20 min. 23 sec.
1955	Cambridge	16 lengths	19 min. 10 sec.
1956	Cambridge	1¼ lengths	18 min. 36 sec.
1957	Cambridge	2 lengths	19 min. 1 sec.
1958	Cambridge	3½ lengths	18 min. 15 sec.

CHANNEL SWIMMERS

THE DISTANCE between Cap Gris Nez in France to Dover in England is some 20 miles, but because of tides a swimmer crossing the Strait has to swim very much farther, the actual distance depending upon when and where he enters the water in relation to the state of the tide, and how long he takes in crossing.

The first Channel swimmer was Capt. Matthew Webb (England), who in 1875 swam from Dover to Calais in 21¾ hours, covering about 40 miles in the effort.

The next swimmer was Thomas Burgess (England), who in 1911 also crossed from Dover to Calais, taking 22 hr. 35 min.

Since 1923 the time has been greatly reduced, some outstanding swimmers and their times being shown below:

		Started	
Swimmer	*Year*	*from*	*Time*
Hassan Abd-el-Rehim (Egypt)	1950	Gris Nez	10 hr. 49 min.*
M. H. Hamad (Egypt)	1951	Gris Nez	12 hr. 12 min.
Roger le Morvan (France)	1951	Gris Nez	12 hr. 13 min.
Hassan Hamad (Egypt)	1951	Gris Nez	12 hr. 12 min.
V. Birkett (England)	1952	Gris Nez	15 hr. 36 min.
Baptiste Periera (Portugal)	1954	Gris Nez	12 hr. 25 min.
M. Hammad (Egypt)	1954	Gris Nez	12 hr. 49 min.
Abdel Heif (Egypt)	1955	Gris Nez	11 hr. 44 min.
Jacques Amyot (France)	1956	Gris Nez	13 hr. 3 min.
C. Forsberg (Gt. Britain)	1957	St. Margaret's Bay	13 hr. 33 min.†
A. Couto (Brazil)	1958	Gris Nez	12 hr. 45 min.

* Fastest official time, France to England.
† Fastest official time, England to France.

MOTOR CYCLING

Highest Speed: 214·40 m.p.h. over flying mile by J. Allen (650 cc. Thunderbird).

One Hour: 127·5 m.p.h. by Piero Taruffi (Italian, Gilera 493 cc.).

CYCLING

100 *miles:* Ray Booty (Britain), 3 hr. 58 min. 28 sec.
1 *hour:* L. Vanderstuyft (Netherlands), 76 miles, 504 yd.

ICE SKATING

500 *metres:* J. Sergeew (U.S.S.R.), 40·9 sec.
1,000 *metres:* C. Thunberg (Finland), 1 min. 28·4 sec.
1,500 *metres:* W. Chaikin (U.S.S.R.), 2 min. 12·9 sec.
3,000 *metres:* A. Huiskes (Holland), 4 min. 40·2 sec.

LAND, WATER, AND AIR RECORDS

Land

THE MAN who holds the distinction of being the fastest on earth is the late John Cobb. In 1939 he averaged 368·85 m.p.h. (fastest run, 370·75 m.p.h.). In 1947 he beat this record, averaging 394·2 m.p.h. (fastest run, 403·2 m.p.h.). Both records were achieved on Bonneville Flat, Utah, U.S.A.

Water

The distinction of being the world's fastest man on water is held by Donald Campbell who, in November 1958, reached an average speed of 248·62 m.p.h. on Coniston Water, N. Lancashire.

The Blue Riband: An award given to the ship which makes the fastest crossing of the North Atlantic. It is held by U.S.S. *United States*, who won it in 1952 with a time of 3 days 10 hours 40 minutes, from Ambrose Light (U.S.) to Bishop Rock Light (Scillies), 2,938 miles. On the return crossing her time was 3 days 12 hours 12 minutes. The award was previously won by R.M.S. *Queen Mary* in 1938.

Air

The top speed in the air has not been disclosed, but it has reached far above the speed of sound (about 760 m.p.h. at sea-level).

A world's official air-speed record was achieved in March 1956 by test-pilot Peter Twiss flying a research aircraft Fairey Delta 2. He averaged 1,132 m.p.h. (top speed on one run, 1,147 m.p.h.).

The world's official altitude record is 63,668 feet (12·06 miles), achieved by Wing Commander W. F. Gibb, D.S.O., D.F.C., in a Canberra bomber on May 4, 1953. It is reported unofficially that a Douglas Skyrocket has reached 80,000 feet.

The longest non-stop flight was made in January 1957 by U.S. Strato-Fortresses : 24,325 miles round the world in 45 hours 19 minutes (about 537 m.p.h.), refuelled four times in flight.

Comet IV records are: Hong Kong to London, 7,925 miles in 16 hr. 16 min.; New York to London, about 3,000 miles, in 6 hr. 7 min. (both records in late 1958).

COMPARATIVE ANIMAL SPEEDS

Golden eagle abt. 150 m.p.h.	Game birds (driven) 50 m.p.h.
Swallow over 100 m.p.h.	Greyhound 38 m.p.h.
African racing	Racehorse 35 m.p.h.
cheetah 70 m.p.h.	Rabbit above 30 m.p.h.
Gobi gazelle over 60 m.p.h.	Pike 20 m.p.h.
Racing pigeon 60 m.p.h.	Salmon 7 m.p.h.

CRICKET RECORDS

Test Matches

Highest Aggregate Innings: 903 for 7 declared, England (*v.* Australia) at the Oval in 1938.

Highest Match Aggregate: 1,981 (S. Africa, 530 and 481; England, 316 and 654 for 5), Durban, 1939.

Highest Scorer: G. Sobers, 365 not out, at Kingston, Jamaica, in 1958; (next highest) Len Hutton, 364, at the Oval in 1938.

Highest Partnership: D. G. Bradman and W. H. Ponsford, 451, at the Oval in 1934.

Other First Class Matches

Highest Aggregate Innings: 1,107, Victoria *v.* New South Wales at Melbourne in 1926.

Highest Scorer: D. G. Bradman, 452 not out, New South Wales *v.* Queensland at Sydney in 1930.

Highest Partnership: Gul Mahomed and V. S. Hazare, 577, Baroda *v.* Holkar in 1947; (next highest) C. L. Walcott and F. M. Worrell, 574, at Trinidad in 1946.

Additional Individual Records

Most Centuries: J. B. Hobbs, 197.

Most Centuries in One Season: Denis Compton, 18 in 1947.

Highest Aggregate: J. B. Hobbs, 61,237; next highest, F. E. Woolley, 58,969.

Most Runs in One Year: Denis Compton, 3,816 in 1947.

Aggregate Wickets: W. Rhodes, 4,188.

Most Wickets in Season: A. P. Freeman, 304 in 1928.

SOCCER RECORDS

Best Scoring Record: James McGrory, 550 (410 in Scottish League, 77 in Scottish Cup, 33 in Glasgow Cup, 18 in Glasgow Charity Cup, and 12 in other first-class matches). Next best: W. R. (Dixie) Dean, 379; Hughie Gallagher, 365; Hugh Ferguson, 362; Steve Bloomer, 352.

League Points Records: First Division, Arsenal, 66 (193 31); Second Division, Tottenham Hotspur, 70 (1919-20); Third Division South, Notts Forest, 70 (1950-51); Third Division North, Doncaster Rovers, 72 (1946-47).

Record League Goals Scored: Aston Villa, 128 goals in 42 League matches (1930-31).

Highest Match Aggregate: Arbroath *v.* Bon Accord, 36-0 (Scottish Cup Tie, 1885).

Longest Match: Stockport County *v.* Doncaster Rovers, 3 hours 45 minutes, 2-2 (March 30, 1946)—failing light stopped play.

Cup Final Venue: 1872, Kennington Oval; 1873, Lillie Bridge, Fulham; 1874 to 1892, Kennington Oval; 1893, Fallowfield, Manchester; 1894, Everton; 1895 to 1914, Crystal Palace; 1915, Old Trafford, Manchester; 1920 to 1922, Stamford Bridge, Chelsea; 1923 to present day, Wembley.

THE OLYMPIC GAMES

THE PRESENT SERIES of Olympic Games began in 189 and have been held in the following places: Athens (1896), Paris (1900 and 1924), St. Louis (1904), London (1908 and 1948), Stockholm (1912), Antwerp (1920), Amsterdam (1928), Los Angeles (1932), Berlin (1936), London (1948), Helsinki (1952), Melbourne (1956).

In the 1956 Games the following events were won by competitors representing Gt. Britain: Equestrian Three-Day Event (team win); Swimming, 100 metres backstroke (Judy Grinham); Boxing, flyweight (T. Spinks), lightweight (R. McTaggart); Steeplechase, 3,000 metres (Chris Brasher); Fencing, women's individual foils (G. Sheen).

The 1960 Games are to be held in Rome.

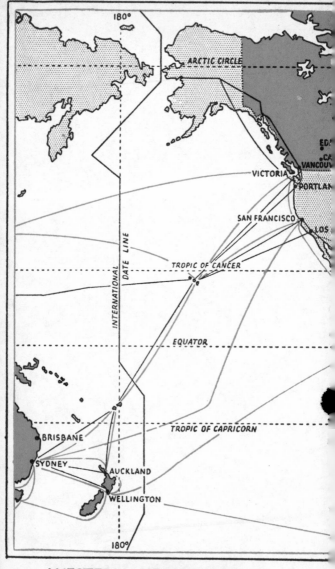

WESTERN HEMISPHERE